Generating Natural Language Descriptions
With Integrated Text and Examples

Generating Natural Language Descriptions With Integrated Text and Examples

Vibhu O. Mittal

Just Research
and
Language Technologies Institute
School of Computer Science
Carnegie Mellon University

LEA

1999

LAWRENCE ERLBAUM ASSOCIATES, PUBLISHERS

Mahwah, New Jersey   London

Lawrence Erlbaum Associates, Inc., Publishers
10 Industrial Avenue
Mahwah, NJ 07430

Cover design by Kathryn Houghtaling Lacey

Library of Congress Cataloging-in-Publication Data

Mittal, Vibhu O.
Generating natural language descriptions with integrated
text and examples / Vibhu O. Mittal
    p. cm.
  Includes bibliographical references and index.
ISBN 0-8058-2414-6 (alk. paper).
ISBN 0-8058-2415-4 (pbk.: alk. paper)
1. Natural language processing (Computer science). 2.
Computational linguistics. I. Title.
QA76.9.N38M58 1998
006.3'5—dc21   98-35087
                                                        CIP

Printed in the United States of America
10   9   8   7   6   5   4   3   2   1

For my parents

Contents

Preface

Most of this research was done as part of my doctoral work at the Information Sciences Institute of the University of Southern California. I was a research assistant in the Explainable Expert Systems (EES) Project, where the goal was to design an expert system shell that would be capable of justifying its decisions and explaining its execution trace in natural language. Procedural knowledge in EES, in the form of plans, was specified in a language called INTEND. INTEND was designed to satisfy the dual goals of being powerful enough to allow the specification of complex problem solving actions and plans, while also facilitating natural language paraphrases of both its syntactic constructs as well as its execution structure. However, initially there was little documentation on INTEND, its grammar, language actions, or their exact semantics. Some of the original developers of the language felt, like all true hackers at heart, that (a) the language could hardly be clearer, with all of its constructs (and the associated syntax) being completely obvious, and (b) for the few exceptional cases that were not, the interpreter source code was always available for perusal. While this user model was usually quite accurate after one had been working on the project for some time, new arrivals to the project often found themselves at sea for a while before they became familiar with INTEND.

Having made the requisite number of mistakes initially in writing INTEND code that refused to work as I thought it should, I decided to work on a dynamic documentation system for INTEND. The goal was that when a user made a mistake, the system would generate appropriate documentation of the relevant construct from the underlying specification. Since the documentation was being generated dynamically, it was guaranteed to be accurate, and furthermore, could be varied to take the context into account. This included factors such as how often the user required help, which constructs had already been presented previously, etc. Since a number of people in the EES Project had previously worked both on paraphrasing program code, as well as varying natural language descriptions based on user models, this was expected to be fairly straightforward. However, it quickly became obvious that a simple paraphrase of the code was not going to be very useful, especially for new users. Rather, what was needed was a description with examples that illustrated the main points. It was this realization that led to the work in this thesis.

Of course, the use of examples in discourse is not a new idea. Examples have been studied extensively since antiquity, and are discussed at length in studies on rhetoric by, among others, Aristotle, Erasmus, Machiavelli, Virgil, Montaigne, Descartes and Pascal. Examples are mentioned as one of the two means of persuasion in Aristotle's *Rhetoric* and *Topics*. Erasmus considered examples to be useful not only as a persuasive device, but also *"to dress it [the argument] up and brighten, expand, and enrich it"* (Erasmus, 1979, p. 607). Even a cursory examination of the early work on rhetoric finds numerous analyses of examples and their uses as a rhetorical device. For instance, extensive discussions by Quintillian, Virgil, and other contemporaries on the different classes/types of examples and their utility in different circumstances can be seen in ancient Latin texts. Other work in rhetoric (e.g., Erasmus' *De Copia*) also discuss aspects of presenting integrated descriptions that include examples. These discuss issues such as the difficulty in interpreting examples without the surrounding context. For instance, Erasmus discusses the death of Socrates, and how that event can be considered in either a positive or a negative light depending on the circumstances (Erasmus, 1979, p. 639).

Of course, our situation when we set out to design a computational system to generate documentation was somewhat different from that of Erasmus and others a few centuries ago. We were concerned, not with examples in rhetoric in general, but in the much more restricted context of concept descriptions. Even in such a restricted domain, we had available for study, large numbers of descriptions (mostly computer documentation) to try and understand how practitioners wrote good descriptions for different subject areas and different levels of intended user expertise. On the other hand, we were also required to build a computational system, and to do so, were required to resolve differences between different proponents of the field and integrate work from other, related areas. The years I spent thinking, experimenting, and writing about this work were enjoyable, exciting, and educational for me ... and the source of many nostalgic memories.

Acknowledgments

Several people played an important role in making this book possible:

People at work:

Cécile Paris: my ex-advisor, mentor, collaborator and now, I'm proud to say, colleague. It is scarcely possible to express my debt to her. She taught me many lessons, not the least of which was how to face seemingly insurmountable odds humbly and cheerfully. Without her, none of this work would have been possible.

Bill Swartout: for getting me to ISI and getting me involved with explanation; my only regret is that I did not get a chance to work with him more closely.

Ramesh Patil: always there to help debug any intricate piece of code, or offer advice on how things should be represented. His detailed suggestions on (re)writing my thesis helped make it far more lucid. His stories about MIT were always entertaining, enlightening, and helped relieve many a dull day.

Paul Rosenbloom: for agreeing to be on my committee at short notice and for being extremely helpful in many ways, ranging from literature pointers to job opportunities. He was also one of the most conscientious people I know. I hope that I can be as considerate to somebody someday as he was to me.

Friends and Family:

My parents, who more than anyone else, have always encouraged me to do pursue my interests, even when these seemed strange, frivolous, or completely off-the-wall. They were always there — usually at the other end of the phone, halfway around the world — willing to listen, support, sympathize, or exult as only parents can. They were understanding enough to never suggest that "it was taking too long" (even though various consular officers asked me why I had not yet finished when I applied every so often for a renewal of my student visa). It is a great gift to be able to count on them for unconditional support. My stay in USA was made much more pleasant, in large part, by having my brother and sister also go through similar experiences in graduate school: I could talk frequently with both Ravi and Madhu, and their encouragement, moral support, regular conversations and holidays with them (and their families) helped some of the years go by quickly.

Sujata: even though we had studied at the same university in India, during much the same time, we first met at USC. Long days and late nights in the "compie room" led to our initial friendship, where Sujata's cheerfulness, enthusiasm and work ethic made her the perfect companion to writing papers, debugging recalcitrant programs, or periodically going out for coffee. My thesis would have taken substantially longer if she had not been there. Having someone to share your feelings with can be a great boon. It is difficult to express the gratitude and love I have for her. By just being there, she made life much better.

My housemates, Subodh, Anand, and Santosh: several years together sharing a house near the USC campus can lead to bonds of friendship not easily forgotten. Together we adjusted to life in Los Angeles, learning how to minimize the "collateral damage" in muggings (carry two wallets, walk in brightly lit areas, avoid gang colors, etc.), while trying to understand the intricacies of each others' research over long, impromptu meals at midnight. Surprise parties that often did not work out, long road trips to meet common friends and old classmates, and extremely intense academic debates on topics ranging from politics to the number system and the definition of life: those were great times.

Yolanda and Kevin: among the nicest people we got to know. Always ready to help. Gave us good advice on a variety of things. It was comforting to talk to them about Ph.Ds, dissertation defenses and job applications. We counted them among our best friends. My one regret is that we knew them for only a year.

Cécile Paris: Last, but certainly not the least. Not only was she an exemplary advisor in many ways, but she was a great friend. I still miss our daily lunches together where we would often try some new salad dressing that she had discovered. My memories of her are a jumbled collage of a great many pleasant occasions. As a teacher, she taught me a lot about research; as a person, her indomitable cheerfulness in the light of personal illness taught me about strength and will-power. I miss her.

To all these people, as well as all the others, who touched my life in a variety of ways, thank you very much. As I look back over the years, I can wish nothing better for other graduate students, than to hope that they have as good a time doing their dissertations as I did!

List of Figures

Chapter 1

Introduction

Good documentation is critical for user acceptance of any system. Sophisticated on-line help facilities based on hypertext or similar retrieval methods are becoming increasingly common. Advances in areas such as knowledge-based systems, natural language generation (NLG) and multi-media now make it possible to investigate the automatic generation of documentation from the underlying knowledge bases. This has several important benefits: it is easily accessible; it avoids frequent problems of inconsistency, as the information presented is obtained directly from the underlying representation; and not the least, it can take the communication context, such as the user, into account.

We make the following claims in this work: examples are necessary in effective explanations; examples cannot just be presented as an afterthought, but must be well-integrated with the accompanying explanation; a text planning mechanism that plans text in terms of communicative goals can be used to generate explanations that integrate text and examples effectively, if the examples are treated as an integral part of the planning process and their effect on the rest of the discourse is taken into account. In this book, we describe the generation of descriptions of the syntax or surface structure for constructs in programming languages. Even though the underlying semantics are not taken into account, the descriptions illustrate important ways in which the text and examples constrain each other.

The work described in this book brings together results from cognitive psychology and education on effective presentation of examples, as well as work on computational generation of examples from intelligent tutoring systems. It also takes into account work in machine learning on computational learning from examples, and a characterization of good examples for this purpose. We present our own analysis of a corpus of instructional and explanatory texts to identify the different ways in which examples interact with the surrounding text. We analyze relevant issues and derive a set of heuristics to generate effective descriptions that integrate both text and examples. We then describe an implemented text generation system that plans presentations of integrated text and examples by taking these factors into account.

The rest of this chapter presents the motivation for the work: (a) the need for documentation in the understanding and user acceptance of complex systems; (b) the use of examples to enhance comprehension, and their use in documentation; and (c) the interaction between the generation of text and examples in a description, as each constrains the other in several ways, and ignoring these interactions and constraints can lead to reduced understandability.

After this background, this chapter concludes by briefly outlining the contributions of the work, and the organization of the book in terms of the chapters that follow.

1.1   The Need for Documentation

> *Documentation of programs is one of the most vital and the most abused aspects of data processing.*
>
> *– P. W. Williams (1977)*
> *U.S. Comptroller-General*

Good documentation is a critical factor in user acceptance of any complex system. The following excerpt from *Time* magazine illustrates the importance of good documentation:

> *Coleco lost $35 million in the fourth quarter last year partly because people flocked to return the initial version of its Adam computer which the company offered for $600. Coleco blamed much of the consumer dissatisfaction on 'manuals which did*

not offer the first-time user adequate assistance' ... *Coleco has reintroduced the Adam complete with a new instruction manual.* (Greenwald, 1984)

There are numerous books and articles on writing good documentation, e.g., (Duin, 1990; Beard and Calamars, 1983; Bell and Evans, 1989; Brockmann, 1990; Brockmann, 1986; Chinell, 1990; Crandall, 1987; Doheny-Farina, 1988; Duffy, Curran, and Sass, 1983; Hastings and King, 1986; Horton, 1991; Maynard, 1982; Morgan, 1980; Pakin and Associates, Inc., 1984; Simpson and Casey, 1988; Stuart, 1984; Yoder, 1986; Tinker, 1963; Willows and Houghton, 1987a; Willows and Houghton, 1987b; Norman, 1988). These deal with issues ranging from the effect of using different typefaces (Tinker, 1963) and the use of everyday metaphors (Norman, 1988; Doheny-Farina, 1988; Hastings and King, 1986), to the effect of illustrations on user comprehension (Willows and Houghton, 1987a; Willows and Houghton, 1987b). It is notable that in spite of differences in their approach and ideology, all these books either stress the need for examples, or make extensive use of examples themselves to convey their point.

Maintaining consistency between the system and the documentation is an important desiderata. As complex systems evolve over time, in response to bug reports, maintenance fixes, and user requests, often the associated documentation fails to keep up with these changes. Such a situation can lead to documentation that is not useful, and worse, even wrong. Documentation generated by the system from the underlying representation of the system can help mitigate this problem of inconsistency between the documentation and the system's representation.

1.1.1 Documentation: The Need for Examples

Examples play an important role in documentation. Consider the two descriptions in Fig. 1.1 for instance. The first description is taken from a book on AI programming (Charniak et al., 1987).[1] The textual explanation for the function is complete (in that it does not omit any facts); however, the second description, with appropriate examples added by

---

[1]The intial sentence enclosed in brackets does not explicitly appear in the book, but the description occurs with other function descriptions, and a generic statement such as this, about all the functions, appears before the group.

```
(GENSYM &optional (PREFIX "G"))
```

[GENSYM is a function call with an optional argument called PREFIX.
It] Returns a new, uninterned symbol, whose print name begins with
PREFIX and ends with a number; the number is incremented with each
call to GENSYM and the default value of PREFIX is reset to whatever is
passed as an argument to GENSYM.

From (Charniak et al., 1987), p. 404.

```
(GENSYM &optional (PREFIX "G"))
```

GENSYM is a function call with an optional argument called PREFIX.
For example:

```
(GENSYM)
(GENSYM "ABC")
```

The function returns a new, uninterned symbol, whose print name begins with PREFIX and ends with a number. For example:

```
(GENSYM "ABC")   ==> #:ABC26
```

The number is incremented with each call to GENSYM.

```
(GENSYM "ABC")   ==> #:ABC27
(GENSYM "ABC")   ==> #:ABC28
```

The default value of PREFIX is reset to whatever string is passed as an
argument to GENSYM.

```
(GENSYM "USC")   ==> #:USC29
(GENSYM)         ==> #:USC30
```

Figure 1.1: Descriptions with, and without, examples.

us, is far more understandable.[2] In this case, the examples highlight points that may not be immediately obvious from the explanation, such as the concatenation of the print name and the number in the output, the fact that the print-name can be different from the actual output, etc.

A number of studies have shown the *need* for examples: a 15 year survey on documentation carried out on behalf of Xerox, Control Data Corporation and Scientific Data Systems found that the lack of adequate numbers of examples was mentioned by users as one of the three most important user complaints (Maynard, 1982).[3] Almost identical results were reported on military documentation by Beard and Calamars (1983). In yet another study, LeFevre and Dixon (1986) found that in 76% of the cases, users looking at documentation consistently skipped over the explanation initially, going directly to the accompanying examples, returning to the explanations only if the examples could not be understood. These studies show that users appreciate examples, and the quality of the documentation or explanation is often judged to be adversely affected by their absence.

1.1.2 Documentation: The Effectiveness of Examples

Empirical studies of effectiveness of examples for comprehension have demonstrated significant differences between explanations with and without examples: a study by Reder, Charney and Morgan (1986) found that the most effective manuals for instructing students on the use of a personal computer were those which contained examples; in one case, when the examples were replaced by "equivalent" textual descriptions (in an IBM PC manual), user comprehension fell to 48% of the previous case when the manual used examples in communication. The speed of learning was seen to increase significantly when examples were included (Charney, Reder, and Wells, 1988; Doheny-Farina, 1988; Reder, Charney, and Morgan, 1986). Books on writing or generating good documentation all stress the need for effective, well structured examples, for instance, (Bell and Evans, 1989; Chinell, 1990; Pakin and Associates, Inc., 1984; Simpson and Casey, 1988; Stuart, 1984; Hastings

---

[2]In an evaluation with about 15 users, we found that *all* of the users found the second description easier to understand compared to the first one.

[3]The other two were that manuals were software oriented rather than function oriented, and that they did not have enough reference aids.

and King, 1986; Horton, 1991).

The use of examples in the comprehension of complex concepts in programming and algebra was studied by a number of researchers, e.g., (Pirolli, 1991; Pirolli and Anderson, 1985; Woolf, 1991; Woolf and McDonald, 1984a; Zhu and Simon, 1987). These studies reflect the importance of examples as an aid to comprehension in educational and instructional contexts. These studies found a need for effective examples in documentation. Most authors writing documentation for tutorial texts recognize this need for examples. Similarly, a system designed to generate documentation on demand from the underlying representation should incorporate examples within the descriptions.

1.2   Examples and the Textual Description

> "**example**, ... *that which is worthy of being put forth*
> *to be imitated or avoided ...*"
>
> – *Dictionnaire de l'Academie (1694)*

Examples are an integral part of any instructional or explanatory process. They help clarify ambiguous definitions and illustrate abstract descriptions. People often use examples to illustrate their point; most text-books include examples in explanations or descriptions of complex concepts. In particular, as we saw previously, examples are *essential* in certain text types, such as instruction manuals and user documentation. Thus, for an explanatory system to be effective, it must be capable of presenting examples to make its point.

Examples alone, however, are not enough. A number of studies have shown that subjects cannot generalize well from examples alone. They have difficulties solving problems that are minor variants of problems thay have seen as examples alone, e.g., (Reed, Dempster, and Ettinger, 1985; Reed, Ernst, and Banerji, 1974; Gick and Holyoak, 1980; Sweller and Cooper, 1985).[4]

---

[4]Some of these negative results can be attributed to the nature of the examples presented to the users — as shown by Pirolli (1991): *structural* examples — examples that showed the form of a *function* — were far more useful to naive students being taught recursion than the *process oriented* examples that explained how recursion ac-

An `assignment` is a construct that tells TₑX to assign a value to a register, to an internal parameter, to an entry in an internal table, or to a control sequence. Some examples of assignments are:

```
\tolerance = 2000
\advance\count12 by 17
\lineskip4pt plus 2pt
\everycr = {\hskip 3pt relax}
\catcode\'@ = 11
\let\graf = \par
\font\myfont cmbx12
```

From (Abrahams, Berry, and Hargreaves, 1990), p. 49.

Figure 1.2: Example of textual elision due to examples.

Matters are not as simple as just presenting both the explanation and the examples. Sweller and his colleagues showed that examples that were not well integrated with the text could make matters worse for the user (Chandler and Sweller, 1991; Sweller and Cooper, 1985; Ward and Sweller, 1990). In the domain of geometry, for instance, they showed how the placement (next to the text, same page, separate page, etc.) of the diagrams that the proof dealt with could substantially affect user comprehension, by distracting the user from the salient points in the description, and cause a deterioration in learning. It is also important that the textual descriptions and the examples complement each other: Chi and her colleagues (1989) showed that naive users understood examples very differently from advanced users. Explanations accompanying examples that did not meet user requirements were not likely to help in understanding the examples, and might even have a negative effect in comprehension. It is therefore important to ensure that both the text and the examples are presented as part of a well-integrated, coherent description that complement each other by taking their interactions, mutual constraints, and the context into account.

---

tually worked; consequently tests in which process oriented examples were presented to introductory users resulted in disappointing results on the effectiveness of examples. Examples cannot be effective without explanatory text, nor can an explanation be effective without accompanying examples.

Examples depend upon the accompanying text (Feldman, 1972), and in turn, affect the actual textual explanation produced (Klausmeier and Feldman, 1975): the information content of the examples and the terms used in conveying that information are dependent on the accompanying description, while the presence of the examples helps the explanation to refer to features and properties of the example to better convey its point. In some cases, the introduction of examples can result in additional textual descriptions being presented; in other cases, some portion of the original textual explanation may be elided. Consider the description in figure 1.2. It describes the assignment operation in TeX. The examples illustrate a number of things which are not mentioned explicitly in the description because they are illustrated in the examples. Some of these are: (a) the variable being assigned a value appears on the left and the value on the right; (b) objects being assigned values can be either global variables, local variables, fonts, or control characters; (c) values being assigned can be either numbers, variables, or expressions to be evaluated; (d) the variable and the value can be separated by "=" or space or nothing at all (the "=" and space, are optional). It is thus clear that the process of incorporating examples is inextricably linked to the process that generates the text.

There is a large body of relevant experimental work on the interaction between examples and their context in education. Researchers have studied the cognitive effects of varying different parameters in the presentation of educational materials in the classroom (Bruner, 1966; Carnine and Becker, 1982; Chi et al., 1989).[5] Much of this work dealt with the construction of conceptual models, studies of attention spans, and the development of effective teaching techniques. None of the studies reported had a computational perspective. However, there are important insights to be drawn from this work. The results on the cognitive effects of presenting contrasting positive and negative examples, the need to present simple examples before complex ones, and the need to vary the examples based on the user corroborate our analysis of the corpus used. The fact that these studies were conducted in different domains (biology, algebra, geometry, etc.) implies that such results

---

[5]Additional references are (Clark, 1971; Engelmann and Carnine, 1982; Feldman, 1972; Feldman and Klausmeier, 1974; Frederiksen, 1984; Gillingham, 1988; Houtz, Moore, and Davis, 1973; Klausmeier, 1976; Klausmeier and Feldman, 1975; Klausmeier, Ghatala, and Frayer, 1974; MacLachlan, 1986; Merrill and Tennyson, 1978; Moore, 1986; Michener, 1978; Rissland, 1978; Tennyson and Park, 1980; Tennyson, Steve, and Boutwell, 1975; Tennyson and Tennyson, 1975; Tennyson, Wooley, and Merrill, 1972).

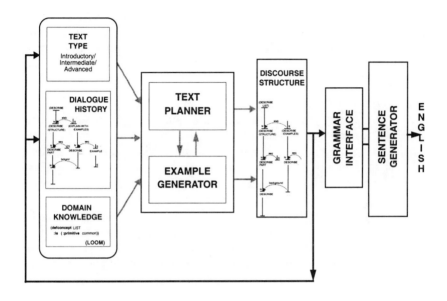

Figure 1.3: A block diagram of the overall system.

are not applicable just to a narrow application (such as programming languages), but are widely applicable.

1.3 The System and the Application Domain

We have seen here that good documentation is an important aspect in user acceptance of a system, that examples are important for good documentation, and that examples cannot just be added to the text because they strongly interact with the accompanying description. To test the validity of the hypotheses that resulted from our corpus analysis, we chose to implement a system in the domain of automatic generation of system documentation. There are many reasons for this choice: (a) automatic documentation is an important application in which to investigate these issues because examples are crucial in documentation and documentation is a critical factor in user acceptance of a system; (b) there is a large body of work on how documentation should be written; (c) a lot of actual material available for our corpus analysis, including numerous examples of different text types (such as introductory and advanced); and (d) we could implement our results within a large software system.

A block diagram of the system is shown in figure 1.3. The system consists of a text planner, an example generator, a grammar interface, and a sentence generator. The system takes a high level communicative goal, such as "describe the concept list"[6] and can generate a description of the type shown in figure 1.4. The system can also be used to generate advanced, reference manual type descriptions of concepts.[7] Reference texts differ from introductory texts in many ways, and these can be handled by the system as well. The system is part of the larger framework in the **E**xplainable **E**xpert **S**ystems Project, EES, (Neches, Swartout, and Moore, 1985; Swartout, Paris, and Moore, 1992; Swartout and Smoliar, 1987), and builds on previous work in text planning and explanation.

1.4   Results

This book is an attempt to synthesize related work on descriptions and examples in psychology, education, the computational generation of examples, and natural language generation together with the results of our corpus analysis. The contributions of this work are:

- an analysis of both the interactions between text and examples, and their mutual constraints by corpus analysis (for instance the fact that examples can cause both deletion and addition of the text around them);

- the identification and analysis of the different features in the ex-

---

[6]The formal notation for specifying such goals is described in chapter 5, where the system is discussed in greater detail.

[7]Introductory and reference texts are the two text types for which the system can currently generate texts. Intermediate texts, which are discussed for the sake of completeness cannot be handled by the system currently, because the underlying semantics of the constructs in our domain are not yet represented.

A list always begins with a left parenthesis. Then come zero
or more pieces of data (called the elements of a list) and a
right parenthesis. Some examples of lists are:

```
(MONKEYS)
(RED PIZZA CARS PLANES)
(2 3 5 11 19)
(5 BLUE 9 FISHES)
```

A list may contain other lists as elements. Given the three
lists:

```
(BLUE ORANGE) (AARDVARKS ELEPHANTS) (FISHES APPLES)
```

we can make a list by combining them all with a parentheses.

```
((BLUE ORANGE)(AARDVARKS ELEPHANTS)(FISHES APPLES))
```

Figure 1.4: A description of the concept list using examples.

---

amples that are important in the context of generation (the position of the examples, the type and amount of information in the
examples, the necessity for prompts in some cases, etc.);

- an improved categorization of example types that takes into account the context of the examples and is computationally imple-
  mentable;

- the identification of the differences between descriptions (in the
  BNF-documentation domain) generated for introductory texts and
  advanced texts;

These claims have been validated by implementation of a text planning
system which generates explanations using the heuristics identified in
this book. The resulting texts not only closely matched with the 'typical'
texts in our corpus, but were in some cases better based on an empirical
evaluation of the cognitive effectiveness of our descriptions.

1.5 Organization of the Book

The book is organized as follows:

Chapters 2 through 4 present the background material, and a discussion of the major issues in the presentation of examples. Chapter 2 presents the background and related work in the use of examples: as aids in Intelligent Tutoring Systems (ITS), work in machine learning on the characteristics of good examples, and on the development of some instructional models that emphasize the use of examples. Chapter 3 discusses the issues that were identified by us as being important in the integration from our corpus analysis. Chapter 4 presents a categorization of example types, necessary in building a computational model.

Chapter 5 presents an overview of an implemented system used in generating descriptions that integrate text and examples. It describes the text planning framework, and the representation of text planning knowledge in the constraints of the plan operators. A brief description of the grammar representation is given, followed by detailed descriptions of how the different examples are generated. This is essential as background for the chapters that follow.

Chapters 6 and 7 illustrate how the system works by describing the generation of different scenarios. These scenarios illustrate certain aspects of the interaction between text and examples, such as textual elision and addition, the effect of negative examples, and so on.

Chapter 8 discusses the effect of the text type on the descriptions. The text type significantly affects the explanations produced, both in terms of the content of the text and examples, as well as in the resulting positions of the examples. A description of a list is generated for two text types (introductory and advanced) to highlight some of these differences.

Chapter 9 presents results from empirical studies on the effectiveness of our heuristics. Portions of the descriptions and the questions asked of the subjects are presented here. In all cases, the issues identified in this book were found to make noticeable differences in the comprehensibility of the descriptions.

Finally, chapter 10 concludes with a discussion of the limitations of the current system, and directions for future work.

Chapter 2

Related Work

This chapter reviews some of the previous research that deals with examples in learning. This work has been primarily conducted in three fields: (a) intelligent tutoring systems (ITS), (b) cognitive science and educational psychology, and (c) machine learning (ML). Work in ITS has been concerned with the generation of examples suitable for education. Work in cognitive science has been focused on factors that affect understanding and human learning from examples. The work in machine learning reviewed here has concentrated on the characterization of good examples from the point of view of efficient learning by a system. The insights gained from this work on ML are relevant to this book because we believe that the characteristics that make examples good for a system to learn from can lead to useful heuristics for human learning.

2.1 Intelligent Tutoring Systems

Examples have been used by intelligent tutoring systems (ITS) in a variety of domains such as mathematics — both in arithmetic, as in the WEST system (Burton and Brown, 1982), as well as in algebra, as in the SETTER system (Baxter, 1989) — legal reasoning, as discussed in the work by Rissland et al. (Rissland, 1983; Rissland, Valcarce, and Ashley, 1984; Rissland and Ashley, 1986), and LISP programming (Reiser, Anderson, and Farrell, 1985). However, these systems concentrated on *finding* appropriate examples for specific aspects of the situation. They did not consider issues involved in presenting the examples as *part of an overall description*. As a result, issues where the context of the examples plays an important role, such as the accompanying explanation, the number of examples and their order of presentation were not considered. These systems were able to do so because of two reasons:

- the descriptions that were generated by these systems were done so using templates that had specific slots for examples, and in some cases, such a template based generation scheme can result in acceptable explanations (Reiser, Anderson, and Farrell, 1985);

- they did not address the explanation issue, but concentrated on the examples in isolation (Baxter, 1989; Rissland, 1983; Rissland, Valcarce, and Ashley, 1984; Rissland and Ashley, 1986).

An exception was the WEST system (Burton and Brown, 1982), that specifically attempted to generate descriptions within a natural language interface. (This system is described further in section 2.1.3.)

Most of the work on finding appropriate examples has concentrated on retrieving and modifying previously stored examples. For example, Rissland (1981) studied the issue of when to *construct vs. retrieve* examples. Later work by Rissland and Ashley led to the identification of 12 important dimensions along which legal examples could be indexed: this was implemented in the HYPO system (Ashley, 1991; Rissland and Ashley, 1986; Rissland, 1983), which used these dimensions (or feature axes) to try to modify a retrieved example. A more general approach was adopted by Suthers and his colleagues in their example generator (Suthers and Rissland, 1988; Woolf, Suthers, and Murray, 1988) where definitions of objects in the domain were annotated with procedural specifications for modifying different features so as to satisfy various constraints.

Our system builds on this work to find appropriate examples for use in the presentation. In the following subsections, we discuss some of these approaches in greater detail and show how they may be used (with appropriate extensions) as a part of an integrated system to generate object descriptions.

2.1.1   CEG: The Constrained Example Generator

Rissland's Constrained Example Generator, or CEG, (Rissland, 1981; Rissland and Soloway, 1980; Rissland, 1980) was one of the first systems to attempt example generation for tutorial purposes. It was designed for use in mathematical domains and could generate examples for requests such as *a list with three elements,* or *a list, such that the first element is also a list.* The system retrieved close matches from a database of examples, and modified them to fit the current goal. It had specialized modules to handle recursive requests such as the second one mentioned above, and could incorporate previously presented examples into the current one.

Rissland's work was concerned with cognitive issues in the use of examples: whether people were more likely to retrieve or construct examples in different situations. In several studies of human protocols, Rissland (1981) was unable to find specific situations where people would do either one or the other; both were equally likely. The CEG system was built to test different example generation algorithms: construction and retrieve-and-modify strategies. The example modification knowledge was stored in specialized routines; it did not attempt to reason about which dimensions to try and modify first (or to avoid trying to modify), or how the features might relate to, and constrain, each other. Since this information was hard-coded in the form of LISP routines, it was difficult to modify the system to study alternative methods and modification strategies.

The system was intended to be a component in a tutoring system (though it was never included in one), and took into consideration factors such as familiarity in the choice of objects in the construction of its examples (such as when constructing a list, the system would try and choose small numbers, like 2 or 3 and try not to repeat them). However, it did not reason about factors such as amount of information to be conveyed per example, possible integration within an explanatory discourse, and so on.

CEG is relevant to our work because it generated examples specifically intended for *tutoring.* Consequently, it included heuristics about the type of components to include in the examples. For instance, when it was necessary to use numbers in an example, rather than use a potentially complex, random number such as 3.14159267, it would attempt to use simpler ones. CEG also incorporated additional heuristics to prevent the presentation of the same example over and over again when asked to present multiple ones. Our example generator uses some of these insights from CEG to generate examples in our framework.

2.1.2   HYPO: Reasoning With Hypothetical Examples

A follow-up to CEG is the HYPO system (Rissland, Valcarce, and Ashley, 1984; Rissland and Ashley, 1986). This system investigates the *retrieve-and-modify* paradigm, and was originally implemented in the domain of trade-rights litigation. It had a knowledge base of domain terms and a specialized knowledge base that contained only examples, the Example Knowledge-Base (EKB).

Given a set of constraints, HYPO could retrieve close examples from the EKB and modify them to fit the situation. It could find positive examples to bolster its case, as well as weaken its opponent's case, with negative examples. The system used 12 predefined features as indices to retrieve the relevant cases. These 12 features were identified as being important from an analysis of real cases. These features were used as an index into the EKB in HYPO; it possessed knowledge on how to modify these 12 parameters to make an example meet specific requirements.

The system was designed to investigate the retrieval and modification of examples in a complex, real-world domain. In actual court cases, the established precedent is considered to be of paramount importance; the system modeled that particular aspect very well. However, it did not address issues other than those covered by the 12 features, and therefore did not address any non-legal issues, such as language, comprehensibility, complexity, and so on. HYPO could reason about the predefined dimensions, but the knowledge about how the dimensions related to one another was encoded in the procedural knowledge, and modification of the system (of any feature's relevance, for instance) was very difficult.

Work on HYPO has looked at issues in the generation of examples based on a general specification of the goal (Aleven and Ashley, 1992; Ashley and Aleven, 1992). The examples (configurations of legal cases) are constructed by putting together individual cases that, when put together, help make an argumentative point. The system uses a KL-ONE representation to find suitable examples. HYPO illustrates how examples can be retrieved (and modified) even in complex, real-world cases.

2.1.3   WEST: Presenting Contextual Examples

One of the most sophisticated game-playing programs built to teach basic mathematical concepts such as addition, subtraction and multiplication was the WEST[1] system (Burton and Brown, 1982).   It generated examples to help illustrate better moves in any given situation. It is notable because it took the context into account while presenting an example. WEST had specialized modules to help it generate suitable natural language phrases in order to interact with the student. The central feature of WEST was its ability to present appropriate examples to help support its criticism if the student made suboptimal moves. These examples were supposed to illustrate the alternative sequence of moves that the student should have explored but did not. If the student made moves that the system considered suboptimal (based on the system's evaluation function), WEST would try and correct the student's high level strategic knowledge by generating a sequence of example moves to illustrate the better strategy.

The system used rules about optimal strategies for the current board position to generate examples for presentation. In general, conjecturing alternative strategies is extremely difficult unless one has a sufficiently closed world, in which case the set of all possible strategies can be characterized. This characterization can be either a generative mechanism, such as a grammar, or an explicit enumeration of all possible alternatives. WEST's world was small enough and closed enough that its designers felt that the latter strategy would work sufficiently well.

WEST is relevant because it is one of the few ITS systems to be extensively field tested. It received high ratings from users. This was credited to the fact that it used natural language to communicate with the users. WEST's success bolsters our position on the use of natural language interfaces. Our approach to designing the documentation system substantially differs from that of WEST. This is because WEST assumed

---

[1]A tutor or coach for the game *"How the West was Won."*

a single user-type, and because of its small domain, it had been possible to enumerate all of its examples *a priori*. This is not possible in domains such as system documentation.

2.1.4 Lessons Learned

The work on ITS illustrates the computational feasibility (CEG, HYPO) and importance (WEST) of generating examples in tutoring. CEG highlighted the issue of using simple elements in tutoring examples. HYPO illustrated the possibility of retrieving and modifying real life, complex examples. WEST demonstrated how the combination of natural language and examples could result in high user acceptance.

The next section describes some of the work in cognitive science and educational psychology that concentrates on effective instructional methods based on the use of examples.

2.2 Cognitive Science and Psychology

There has been a tremendous amount of work on examples done in both cognitive science and educational psychology. Examples have always been regarded as important in instruction; Klausmeier (1976) hypothesized that if definitions alone were presented (without accompanying examples), "the child runs the danger of merely memorizing a string of verbal associations, rather than understanding the concept." In this section, we discuss some of the studies relevant to this work. (Other studies that help corroborate our findings, while not discussed here, will be cited appropriately.) These studies serve as the basis for some of the heuristics used in our system. For instance, the Direct Instruction Model (DIM), described next, discusses different ways of presenting instructional material and specifically deals with sequences of examples. Cognitive Load Theory (CLT) deals with directing the cognitive resources toward activities that are relevant to learning; some of the work on distraction by the wrong placement of examples and text (and figures and text) is directly relevant to our work.

2.2.1 The Direct Instruction Model

The *Direct Instruction Model*, or DIM, (Bruner, 1966; Engelmann and Carnine, 1982; Moore, 1986) is an instructional-design theory that is concerned with the "creative application of empirically verified instructional principles to improve the effectiveness of instruction across a wide range of cognitive outcomes." DIM is mad eup of four components that specify:

1. the kind of experiences that pre-dispose a student towards learning,

2. the form and structure of knowledge,

3. the most effective sequence in which to present the material, and

4. the nature and pacing of rewards and punishments in the process.

DIM is a prescriptive model that does not *a priori* determine educational or training goals, but sets out a means to accomplish them, once they have been established. Most importantly, DIM categorizes knowledge types in order to determine the most efficient means of presenting each category to the user. There are three categories into which knowledge can be arranged: (a) facts, (b) correlations, and (c) cause-effects. Each of these categories is further subdivided by Bruner (1966) as follows:

- **Facts (Basic Forms):**
    - noncomparatives (single dimensioned concepts, such as the color green and the number 5.)
    - comparatives (in a single dimension, such as larger, heavier, brighter and so on.)
    - nouns and multi-dimensional concepts (such as a car, a shoe, and a book.)

- **Correlations (Joining Forms):**
    - transformations ($F(x) \rightarrow y$)
    - feature relationships ("when it rains, the leaves get wet")

- **Cause-Effects (Complex Forms):**
    - cognitive problem solving routines
    - communications about events (fact systems)

Each of these subtypes is then analyzed to see how presentations of that particular form should be made in instructional contexts. DIM contains specifications that must be considered during *initial* instruction through examples. These are directly relevant in this research. For instance, it contains warnings such as: "A concept cannot be taught through the presentation of only one example. Positive examples alone are not sufficient, negative examples should be presented as well."

The DIM methodology is important because, unlike most other models in instructional design, it describes the generalization learned by the reader in terms of the features presented in the examples. (Other models do so in terms of the internal processes of the user.) This allows the DIM model to be applied to a computational system where the initial presentation is planned based on the features of the concept to be described, rather than a detailed cognitive model of the user's learning abilities. Within DIM, individual differences in users are seen as irrelevant to the design of the instruction. Learning outcomes are determined not by constructs such as the development stage, but by features of the knowledge (in terms of the specific sets of examples) communicated to the user. Our system makes use of the directives in DIM (such as the presentation of a pair of contrasting examples to illustrate some features) to plan the presentation.

2.2.2 Adaptive Presentation Strategies

Adaptive presentation strategies, in contrast to the Direct Instruction Model, attempt to vary the presentation based on the user's response. Work in this area of research has mostly focused on various aspects of concept acquisition through the use of different instructional strategies in classroom instruction, as in (Park and Tennyson, 1980; Tennyson, Wooley, and Merrill, 1972; Park and Tennyson, 1986; Merrill and Tennyson, 1977; Merrill and Tennyson, 1978; Tennyson and Park, 1980; Tennyson, Steve, and Boutwell, 1975; Tennyson and Tennyson, 1975; Carnine, 1980a; Carnine, 1980b; Carnine and Becker, 1982).

Adaptive presentation strategies are based on the hypothesis that concept learning is a two-stage process: conceptual knowledge is formulated first, followed by development of procedural knowledge (Tennyson, Chao, and Youngers, 1981; Tennyson, Youngers, and Suebsonthi, 1983; Anderson, 1987). Adaptive presentation strategies dictate that example presentations should be sensitive to error patterns in these two learning phases: if the learner has just been presented initial information about a concept, the examples should be oriented towards learning the declarative, conceptual form. On the other hand, if the learner has already been presented with the conceptual information, 'interrogative'[2] examples should be presented. Results have shown that this adaptive instructional strategy was superior to the fixed selection strategy in terms of both post-test and retention performance (Park and Tennyson, 1986).

Presentations in which the number and order of examples were varied based on the user response were also seen to be useful in enhancing comprehension (Park and Tennyson, 1980). An experiment to test the discrimination ability found that examples should be presented that cause the learner to understand one discriminant before presenting further examples that deal with other discriminating features of the concept. Thus, if succeeding examples are presented in reference to the classification of the response, rather than in a predetermined (response insensitive) order, the number of examples could be minimized.

This model underlines the need to present appropriate number of examples in the right order, as well as with the correct level of difficulty. If the learner's comprehension can be taken into account during the presentation process, adapting the examples from a declarative form initially (simple positive examples), to an interrogative form (negative, as well as positive examples that highlight discriminating features) as the learner gains familiarity with the concept, can help minimize the number of examples that need to be presented.

---

[2] Interrogative examples are examples that highlight discriminant features. Such features can be used to categorize concepts in membership classes, and to answer questions about whether an instance belongs to a particular concept class or not.

2.2.3 Cognitive Load Theory

Cognitive Load Theory (Chandler and Sweller, 1991; Sweller and Cooper, 1985; Ward and Sweller, 1990) suggests that effective instructional material facilitates learning by directing cognitive resources toward activities that are relevant to learning, rather than toward preliminaries to learning. Thus, the presentation of unnecessary information (even information that was useful, but nonessential, such as a commentary on a figure) had deleterious effects on the learning process. On the other hand, a separation in the presentation of independent sources of information did not detract from comprehensibility. Thus, two unrelated pieces of information could be presented at different places, or different times, with no loss in user comprehension.

On the other hand, separation of related sources of information, such as explanations and diagrams, or text and examples, resulted in reduced comprehension when compared to their integrated presentation. These studies indicate that there is a need to present different sources of information, such as text and examples, appropriately: physically close, mutually referent, if they are related and complementary; explicitly separated, or annotated as being independent, if the examples and text are not mutually referent and are not necessary for understanding each other.

2.2.4 Examples and Explanations

In an effort to study the utility of examples in complex subjects such a recursion (in programming languages), Pirolli and Anderson (1985) studied a group of 19 students learning to program.[3] The success of their attempts was dependent upon how well they understood the working of the examples. The subjects, all novices in programming, were split into two groups; both groups were given explanations with examples that illustrated the concept of recursion. One group was given an explanation of recursion in terms of the *structure* of the examples — how it was *written*: the fact that the terminating condition was written before the recursive call, and so on — while the other group was given a *process* oriented explanation of recursion — how the example

---

[3]Evidence of the popularity of examples can be seen in that 18 of the 19 students immediately attempted to use previously seen examples to write code.

worked. The examples in both the explanations were identical, whereas the textual explanations accompanying the examples were different.

The group which was given the explanation in terms of the structure fared much better than the other group which was given process-oriented explanation (in terms of time taken for understanding). In the case of advanced users, however, (users with knowledge and experience of related concepts), on presentation of the same examples and descriptions, the group that was given the process-oriented explanations fared better. Given that the examples were the same, it is clear that the differences in the comprehension and learning time were due to the accompanying explanation.

To investigate the importance of explanations, Chi et al. (1989) analyzed self-generated explanations of students working through complex examples in the domain of mechanics. Because examples typically contain a series of unexplicated actions, self-explanations are important in understanding the significance of the example. The study found that good and poor students used the examples in different ways: good students tend to refine and expand conditions for the actions in the example solutions, and link them back to the principles in the textual explanations; poor students do not generate sufficient self-explanations and rely very heavily on previously seen examples when attempting to solve further problems. This study shows that in the case of naive students, the explanations that accompany the examples must encourage the linkage between the given example and the general principles.

These studies emphasize the importance of presenting a textual explanation along with the examples to help clarify and disambiguate difficult or important features in the examples.

2.2.5 Summary

Each of the four approaches discussed — DIM, Adaptive Presentation, Cognitive Load Theory and combining examples and explanations — has important consequences for the comprehensibility of generated descriptions. The presentation directives in DIM are useful because a computational system can have, at best, a sketchy model of the learner's cognitive state. At the same time, it can have extensive information about the features and attributes of the concept it wishes to present. Adaptive Presentation techniques are important because the system has to generate for different user types with differing backgrounds; the system must also be responsive to the context as well as the previous interaction. Cognitive Load Theory, and the studies on explanations with examples, emphasize the need to physically as well as conceptually integrate the related components while explicitly separating unrelated ones. As we shall see later, this becomes essential in cases where exceptional (or anomalous) examples are presented by the system.

2.3 Machine Learning

Examples have always been used in machine learning. Systems have been implemented to test various theories, and computational results have been derived. Inductive machine learning from examples and Explanation Based Learning (EBL) represent two of the approaches that have been studied in this area. In this section, we review some work in machine learning pertinent to this work. The work reviewed here deals with the characterization of good examples for machine learning. There are similarities between machine learning and cognitive learning (and some of the work in machine learning is inspired by cognitive analyses, such as SIERRA, for instance), and the hope is that examples that are good for machine learning have characteristics that are beneficial for learning in people as well.

Particularly relevant is the work in computational learning theory, where it has been shown that factors such as the type of examples presented, the order in which they are presented, and whether the target concept contains disjunctions, can significantly influence the resources required for generalizing to a concept (Valiant, 1984; Angluin, 1987), and the number of examples that are required to do so (Ling, 1991; Rivest and Sloan, 1988). Similar results hold in cognitive studies of learning, where the limited amount of short-term memory can determine which presentation sequences are likely to be effective (Anderson, Kline, and Beasley, 1980; Anderson and Matessa, 1990). In the next section, we describe some of the earlier work on learning from examples for illustration.

2.3.1   Learning from Near-Misses — ARCH

One of the earliest systems to learn from examples, the ARCH program (Winston, 1975; Winston et al., 1983), learned generalized structural[4] descriptions from a series of examples. It identified the notion of a "near-miss" as being an important concept in learning. These near-miss examples were examples that differed from positive examples in only one feature. When a negative example differs from the current understanding in more than one feature, the learner cannot determine which (or both) of these differences is the critical one. This can lead to considerable search and false refinement. The program used these near-misses to reason about *mandatory* and *inconsequential* relations in this model[5] — the system learned to distinguish these based on the classification of the examples it was shown. ARCH was among the first programs to emphasize the quality of examples as a factor in its learning process.

ARCH is relevant to this work in several ways: it was the first attempt to characterize good examples in the learning process. The concept of *near-misses* — which exists in DIM, and is expressed as the need to present a pair of contrastive examples — and the stress on the presentation sequence of examples are both important criteria that must be adhered to by the system.

2.3.2   Version Spaces

Mitchell's (1982) *version space* approach presents one of the first computational accounts of how negative examples can help constrain the search space of possible generalizations. The approach involves representing and revising the set of all hypotheses that are describable within the framework and are consistent with the observed examples. Two sets are used to represent the hypothesis space: S, which represents the *most specific* generalizations and G, which represents the *most general* specializations consistent with the examples. S and G are updated with each example. When the two sets are identical, the

---

[4]*Structural* descriptions portray objects as consisting of various components that have different relationships defined between them; *attribute* descriptions, on the other hand, list only global properties of the object, for instance, its height, weight or color.

[5]These are similar to the *critical* and *variable* features defined in educational psychology.

system stops because any further examples would not contribute new information. The version space approach requires the ability to order generalizations by specificity and by direct examination. The advantage of the version space approach lies in the fact that G summarizes the implicit information in the negative examples (by bounding the maximum level of generality) and S summarizes the implicit information in the positive instances. This representation of the version space in terms of G and S allows the algorithm to process examples without explicitly storing the training examples for later consideration.

The results from version-spaces illustrate the *necessity* of negative examples in the learning process, rather than just their desirability: the G set is specialized based on the negative examples seen by the system. Similarly, the use of negative examples can help learners prune their mental hypothesis spaces.

2.3.3 Generating Examples — LEX

LEX (Mitchell, Utgoff, and Banerji, 1983) was a system designed to investigate the acquisition of problem-solving heuristics in the domain of symbolic integration. LEX learned heuristics by generating practice problems to solve, attempting to solve them, and then generalizing from the problem-solving experience. The rate of learning was thus dependent on the nature of problems that LEX attempted to solve. LEX used the version space approach to learn new knowledge. The two important points of LEX were: (a) it possessed heuristics to generate example problems, and (b) it had perfect knowledge of the internal state of the learner.

One of the heuristics used by LEX in generating example problems was to generate a problem that would allow the refinement of some existing, partially learned domain heuristic. To do this, it would select a partially learned heuristic, find a previously solved problem that matched it, and then minimally modify the problem until it no longer matched the heuristic completely. Thus, LEX generated near-misses, based on this heuristic, for its own learning mechanism.

LEX is very relevant to this work because it was concerned with the issue of generating good examples for the system to solve. To this end, it generated near-miss problems; the difference between LEX and a human teacher is that LEX *knew* the exact state of the learner, and could therefore target its problems to refine partial heuristics.

2.3.4 Importance of Example Sequences — SIERRA

SIERRA (VanLehn, 1987) is a machine learning system that was inspired by class-room observations. Thus, characterizations of good examples for SIERRA are based on good examples in classroom situations.
Van Lehn (1987) found that people tend to regard as significant the order in which the examples are presented to them. SIERRA, a computational learning system , was among the first to try and make use of the
sequencing assumption: that the examples presented to it had been
generated by someone who had taken the sequencing into account.
SIERRA used this assumption to bridge gaps in the example sequences
presented to it by considering the examples around the gap. The use
of this assumption allowed SIERRA to significantly reduce the number
of examples required to learn a procedure; previous systems had assumed that each of the training examples presented were independent
of one another; they considered each example in isolation, ignoring information such as its position in a sequence, its neighboring examples
— cues that are usually valuable in real teaching situations.

This discussion on SIERRA is relevant because it underlines the fact
that the presentation of examples in an appropriate sequence can greatly
reduce the number of examples required to learn the concept.

2.3.5 Machine Learning and Documentation

There is an interesting parallel between machine learning and documentation. The requirements in two approaches in machine learning
from examples correspond to two different text types in documentation.
One approach to learning from examples is *induction*, which assumes
minimal background domain knowledge, as discussed in (Holland et
al., 1987; Michalski, 1983). The other is *Explanation Based Learning*,
or EBL (Mitchell, Keller, and Kedar-Cabelli, 1986; DeJong and Mooney,
1986), which requires the presence of a strong domain theory. Induction often assumes no prior knowledge of the concept and can require a
great many number of examples to generalize. EBL, on the other hand,
with its strong domain theory, can sometimes learn from just a single,
complex example. We noticed that introductory texts meant for naive

users (with little or no domain knowledge) used a large number of examples to explain a concept, whereas reference materials targeted towards advanced users (with significant amounts of domain knowledge, as in EBL) had far fewer, and more complex examples.

2.4   Discussion

Much of the work on learning from examples in each of the three fields discussed above (cognitive science, intelligent tutoring systems, and machine learning) has significant implications for each other. For instance, the importance of "near-misses" has been emphasized in both cognitive psychology and machine learning; the importance of presenting minimal irrelevant features and ordering the presentation sequence have also been studied in both fields. Computational complexity results on learning disjunctions in machine learning parallel some of the results in cognitive studies in children.

Surprisingly few tutoring systems have attempted to make use of examples as one of their teaching strategies. This may be because for example presentations to be effective, there are many other issues that must also be addressed before practical systems can be designed to take advantage of this strategy (issues such as the type and amount of information to be presented in each example, the description, their placement, and so on.). Also, unless the examples used are appropriate for the context, they can be detrimental, rather than helpful, in user comprehension.

Our system synthesizes the insights from previous work and builds on them: it uses the results from ITS to find and construct good examples; results from cognitive science and educational psychology to plan effective and comprehensible presentations; and results from machine learning in modifying examples to construct near-misses and use them in presentation sequences.

In the following chapter, we discuss the issues that arise in the generation of integrated descriptions with both text and examples.

Chapter 3

Issues in the Integration of Text and Examples

*Examples, like eyeglasses, blur everything
that they do not make more clear.*

– Anonymous

We have argued in chapter 1 that documentation is far more effective when it contains well-integrated examples. Many issues must be addressed before a systematic account can be developed and a system can be implemented to generate such descriptions: this chapter discusses these in more detail. These issues were identified based on a corpus analysis, as well as a synthesis of previous studies in cognitive science and educational psychology.

3.1   Corpus Analysis

We studied a large number of descriptions in different manuals, books, help materials, and online documentation to identify the interactions between text and examples and help isolate relevant issues in their integration. The corpus consisted of books about LISP (Meehan, 1979; McCarthy et al., 1985; Novak, 1985; Shapiro, 1986; Steele Jr., 1984;

Tatar, 1987; Touretzky, 1984; Charniak et al., 1987; Norvig, 1992; Keene, 1989; Wilensky, 1983; Friedman and Fellesisen, 1987; Winston and Horn, 1984; Lucid, 1990), as well as other programming languages: Postscript (McGilton and Campione, 1992; Braswell, 1989), TEX (Knuth, 1990; Knuth, 1979; Abrahams, Berry, and Hargreaves, 1990; Borde, 1992), C (Perry, 1992; Vetterling et al., 1990; Harbison and Steele, 1993), and Unix (UNIX Documentation, 1986; Waite, Martin, and Prata, 1983; Stevens, 1990). Each of these publications is well regarded as either a good textbook or a definitive reference manual in its area. Some of these books such as (McGilton and Campione, 1992; Borde, 1992; Perry, 1992; Vetterling et al., 1990), explicitly attempt to explain by using examples.

The availability of multiple books and publications on the same language allowed us to examine various descriptions of the same concept. In addition, we had available publications which were intended either for use as reference manuals by advanced users, or as introductory material meant for naive users. This proved invaluable, as the differences between these two genres is quite significant. In this chapter, we discuss some of the issues raised by our corpus analysis. When discussing each of these issues, we attempt to reference related work in cognitive psychology, to show that some of these issues had already been remarked on, though usually in isolation, rather than as part of a set of criteria that determine the effectiveness of the presentation.

3.2   Issues in Integration

It is essential when planning an explanation that involves examples to pick the examples carefully to fit in the accompanying text. A bad example can be worse than no example. However, choosing the correct example is not sufficient either, because care must be taken to present it in a way that can be understood easily. This implies that the accompanying explanation must also complement the example. As Pakin observes:[1]

> Examples and illustrations support and amplify verbal explanations. They help make concepts specific and show how

---

[1]Underlining is ours.

things look and work ... <u>Simply including examples and
illustrations does not, however, improve documentation.</u> To
be effective, each illustration must be an essential piece of
documentation — well-planned, carefully prepared, prop-
erly labeled, and easily understood. The text should refer
to the example specifically.

(Pakin and Associates, Inc., 1984), p. 9.

Examples cannot be generated in isolation, but must form an integral part of the description, supporting and complementing the surrounding text. A number of issues arise in generating descriptions and
examples in a coordinated, coherent fashion, such that they complement and support each other. These issues are:

1. When should an example be generated?

2. How is each example generated? Is it retrieved from a knowledge
   base, or is it constructed? What attributes guide the construction
   and retrieval processes?

3. What information should each example contain? How does it relate to the explanatory text? How many examples should be used?
   Should the information to be communicated be divided across a
   number of examples, and if so, how?

4. What order should examples be presented in, if more than example is to be presented? Does this order affect the structure of the
   accompanying text?

5. How should the example be positioned with respect to the explanation? Should the example be *within* the text, *before* it, or *after*
   it?

6. When should *prompts*[2] be generated and how should they be indicated?

7. What should be contained in the *descriptive component* of the explanation?[3]

---

[2]Prompts are attention-focusing devices such as arrows, marks, or additional text,
associated with examples.

[3]Descriptions occurring in different text-types are often quite different. In this work,
we are mainly concerned with the differences between introductory texts and advanced
texts.

8. Are there different types of examples? If so, what, if any, are the consequences of membership in a particular category? Do different types of examples need to be presented differently?

9. Does the *text type* play a role in the description? Does it place constraints on the textual explanation, the examples, or both?

10. How does the *type* of information (concept *vs.* relations) being communicated affect the explanation? textual explanation, examples, or both?

We discuss the first six issues in turn in this chapter. Issue 7 will be discussed in the context of the other issues, as well as when the issue of the text type (issue 9) is dealt with in chapter 8. Issue 8 is described in detail in chapter 4. The last issue on the knowledge type is discussed briefly at the end of this chapter.

3.3   When should an example be presented?

An important question to address before a system can be implemented to effectively use examples in descriptions is the question of when it should attempt to use an example. The presentation of examples can be either system– or user-initiated.

The system can decide to include an example as part of its description, to illustrate one or more features. This can be due to the fact that the explanation strategy being followed by the system specifies the need for examples. This is the case for certain text types, such as online help manuals (these manuals have a fixed format of descriptions that are invariably followed by examples), and for certain types of concepts, such as abstract concepts. Exactly when an example is generated depends upon both the concept being described and the text type. This will be explained in detail later, in chapter 6.

The user can initiate example generation by signalling the need for an example in confusion over a complex or abstract definition. Indications of confusion can be responses such as "Huh?" or repeated requests for help on the same topic. Both Woolf and McDonald (1984a) and Moore's PEA system (Moore, 1995) followed a strategy whereby the system would present an example if the user did not indicate an understanding after presentation of a definition.

3.4 Retrieval vs. Construction of Examples

Suitable examples need to be found before they can be used in a description. Examples can either be retrieved from a predefined example database and modified to suit the given situation, or constructed in response to a specified goal. HYPO (Ashley and Aleven, 1992; Ashley, 1991; Rissland and Ashley, 1986; Rissland, Valcarce, and Ashley, 1984) is an example of a system that took the former approach (retrieval). As discussed in chapter 2, it had twelve pre-defined dimensions along which the feature values could be modified to make the example specific to the given situation. So did the generator by Suthers and Rissland (1988). The Constrained Example Generator (CEG) by Rissland (Rissland, 1980; Rissland, 1981) took the other approach, investigating how examples could be constructed by putting together simpler examples.

From a cognitive perspective, it is not yet clear which method is preferred in different circumstances. Protocol analyses by Rissland (in the geometry domain) demonstrated that people were equally likely to do either one (Rissland, 1981). Computationally, there are advantages and disadvantages for both approaches: retrieval and modification implies an efficient indexing scheme into a database of example instances and adequate rules to modify the example to fit the given situation. This approach relies on the assumption that a close match will be available, that modification will be relatively inexpensive and that will result in an appropriate example. However, in some cases, this approach may prove to be more expensive than constructing the example from scratch (Rissland, 1981). Construction of an example, on the other hand, assumes the availability of sufficient knowledge to assemble an example by putting together its components in the correct manner; this requires some knowledge of how the different features of an instance interact and contribute to it being a good or a bad example. Modification can often be achieved with less background knowledge than construction, because the system need only change certain feature values. There has been considerable work on modification in Case Based Reasoning on adapting cases for particular situations; some of these issues were discussed in (Hammond, 1990; Kambhampati, 1990b; Kambhampati, 1990a; Veloso and Carbonell, 1990; Cook, 1989; Mostow, 1989; Stanfill and Waltz, 1986; Schank and Riesbeck, 1981).

It is likely that a flexible system will need both retrieval as well as construction capabilities.

3.5　The Number of Examples

Studies have shown that user comprehension is enhanced when the
message contains a minimum number of irrelevant features, allowing
the user to focus on the important aspects of the message. This also
holds if the message is in the form of examples (Ward and Sweller,
1990). This maxim is particularly important for example presentation
because examples are concrete instances, bristling with detail. It is
usually not possible to construct examples without all the associated
low level details, as some of these details are required for the example
to have its illustrative power. For instance, the definition of a function
(in most programming languages) requires the specification of three
components: The function name, the parameters of the function, and
the body of the function. However, examples of a function will contain
not just these three conceptually important components, but also low
level syntactic requirements. Examples illustrating this are shown in
figure 3.1.

In the first case, the example illustrates the use of defun as a means
of defining a new function name. To do so, the example also presents a
number of features not mentioned in the definition: the fact that there
are a number of parentheses, the function has parameters, a documentation string, and a body that references the parameters, and so on.
The second example illustrates a procedure that does symbolic computation. As in the previous case, a number of details necessary for the
example to work are not mentioned in the description. For instance,
the use of the CADR function to retrieve the second element of a list as
an atom, and then the use of the LIST function to create a new list. In
the third case, the example (from the programming language PASCAL),
facts such as the statement separator is a semi-colon, the program ter-
minator is a period, the use of the keywords 'begin' and 'end,' and so
forth.

Each example of a concept will necessarily include some features or
attributes of the concept. These features can be classified into two categories, depending on their role:

- **critical features:** features that are *required* for the example to

The special form defun stands for "define function." It is used here to define a new function called last-name.

> (**defun** last-name (name)
>   "Select the last name from a name
>   represented as a list"
>   (first (last name)))

From (Norvig, 1992), p. 12.

Consider an example of a procedure that does symbolic computation, rather than a numerical one. This procedure exchanges the first and second elements of a two element list:

> (**defun** exchange (pair)
>   (list (cadr pair) (car pair)))   ; *Reverse elements*

From (Winston and Horn, 1984), p. 42.

When a program has more than one statement, each one is executed in the order it appears. For example:

> **program** *SecondRun* (*output*);
> **begin**
>   *writeln* ('Hello. I love you.');
>   *writeln* ('How about lunch?')
> **end.**

From (Cooper and Clancey, 1982), p. 8.

Figure 3.1: Examples often contain many other details.

be an instance of the concept being illustrated. For instance, the definition of a function in LISP *must* begin with the left parenthesis, followed by the keyword defun, followed by the function name and a list (possibly empty) of the parameters. If either of these is missing, the example is not of a function.

- **variable features:** features that can change within an example without causing the example to not be an example of the concept being illustrated. For instance, the name of a function and the names and number of parameters are among are variable features of a function definition. Their presence is critical, but their actual value is not.

It is essential that the user grasp this difference in the nature of the features. Thus, the system must take this factor into account when presenting examples. To minimize confusion, the system must present examples that highlight specific features and their type (critical or variable) clearly. This can be done, for instance, by presenting pairs of examples, that are identical in all respects, except for the feature being illustrated. This implies that the pair of examples that attempts to emphasize a critical feature will be a *positive-negative*[4] example pair; the pair that emphasizes the variable nature of another feature will be either a *positive-positive* or a *negative-negative* pair. Because a concept can have a number of critical and variable features, the clearest possible presentation would have at least one pair of examples for each feature. However, this may not always be possible because of restrictions by the text type. This is reflected in the data, where descriptions in advanced, reference manual type texts have very complex examples with a large number of features. Consider, for instance, the examples in figure 3.2.

The first example, from (Harbison and Steele, 1993), illustrates the fact that in the C programming language: (a) type declarations can define a new type, (b) specify that a variable is of that type, (c) any number of variables can be specified to be of that type, etc. The second example from Steele (1984) illustrates multiple different aspects of the format statement in LISP: the fact that it can be used to combine symbols into strings, be used to select from different parameters passed to it, some directives may be recursive, and so on.

---

[4]A *positive* example is an example of the concept being illustrated. A *negative* example is *not* an example of the concept being illustrated.

An enumerated type in C is a set of integer values represented by identifiers ... [number of lines deleted] ...
For example:

```
enum fish { trout, carp, halibut }
     my_fish, your_fish ;
```

From (Harbison and Steele, 1993)

[A long description of various options that a format statement can take appears here, and has not been reproduced.]

```
(format nil "~@? ~D" "<~A ~D>" "Foo" 5 14 7)
⟹      "<Foo 5> 14"
```

From (Steele Jr., 1984)

Figure 3.2: Examples in advanced, reference manual type texts are
complex and multifeatured.

The number of examples is also dependent on the intended user: the number of critical features the user can be expected to recognize and assimilate from each example. For an introductory text, each example should contain as few features as possible, to ensure that the user is able to recognize them (Klausmeier, 1976; Feldman, 1972; Clark, 1971). On the other hand, an advanced user is likely to understand examples containing three to four features without significant difficulty.

The number of examples will thus depend on the text type, as well as the total information content to be conveyed. Studies have suggested that there is a maximum number of examples before the user loses attention. Clark (1971) suggested that four examples were optimal to explain a concept to the user in most cases; more than four together resulted in loss of attention. Feldman and Klausemeier found that the number of examples required depended on (a) the number of attributes, (b) the level of abstraction, and (c) the student's learning characteristics; no fixed, optimal number was suggested (Feldman, 1972; Klausmeier and Feldman, 1975). Markle and Tiemann (1969), suggested that an "observation of the critical and variable attributes" to determine the number of examples was required.

3.6 Order of Presentation of Examples

Given that there may be a number of examples to be presented, their presentation sequence is important. Psychological studies show that the order of presentation of the examples plays an important role in comprehension. Feldman (1972) reported that sequencing was most effective when positive and negative examples were paired together. Houtz et al. (1973) suggested that sequencing positive examples and *minimally differing* positive and negative examples together was the most effective sequencing strategy; Klausmeier et al. (1974), Litchfield et al. (1990), Markle and Tiemann (1969), and Tennyson et al. (1975), reported essentially the same (latter) conclusions.

Ordering the examples can be done on at least two levels:

1. **feature level:** at the 'macro' level, the order in which different features of the concept are to be illustrated using examples.

2. **example level:** at the 'micro' level, the order *within* a set of examples illustrating a feature.

Empirical studies show that presenting easily understood examples before presenting more difficult ones has a significant beneficial effect on the listener (Carnine, 1980b). A set of examples illustrating the importance of ordering based on complexity are shown in figure 3.3. This ordering is also suggested by the *Principle of End-Weight* in linguistics (Giora, 1988; Werth, 1984), where sequencing the presentation of easily understood information before the presentation of inferred or unknown (relatively more difficult) information is recommended. Thus, when describing a concept, the simpler features should be presented before the more complex ones. The determination of the complexity of a particular feature is domain dependent. In our domain of programming languages, an indication of the complexity of a particular symbol in the grammar can be obtained by estimating the total number of unique examples that could be generated to illustrate that symbol. In a sense, the greater the number of examples possible, the greater its complexity.[5] This will be explained in more detail in section 5.3.5.

Within a set illustrating a particular feature, the importance of sequencing becomes even more evident because of the implicit information that the sequence can be used to convey. The order of presentation is an important means of focusing the reader's attention. Sequencing can be used to highlight the critical features by presenting pairs of positive and negative examples, and emphasize the variable features by presenting different positive examples. Consider for instance, the examples in figure 3.4. The first two pairs of examples illustrate the point that atoms and numbers are not lists unless they are enclosed in parentheses. The next three examples show that *symbols* or *numbers*, or both, can be elements in a list, and finally, the last example shows that a list can also be made up of other lists. These points would have been much less obvious if the examples had been presented as in figure 3.5, because the reader would have to realize the similarity between different examples and contrast them on his or her own.

Thus, a *critical* feature can best be illustrated through a *pair* of

---

[5]The actual computation of the complexity uses a heuristic that takes into account the number of explicitly defined terminal symbols that a symbol can make use of; this prevents the nonterminal 'integer-number,' for instance, from being assigned a complexity value of infinity.

Mathematical operators in TₑX can have limits. The lower
limit is specified as a subscript, and the upper limit as a
superscript. Examples of operators with limits are:

```
$$\bigcap_{k=1}^r (a_k \cup b_k)$$
```

produces

$$\bigcap_{k=1}^{r} (a_k \cup b_k)$$

while

```
$${\int_0^\pi \sin^2 ax\,dx} = {\pi \over 2}$$
```

produces

$$\int_0^{\pi} \sin^2 ax\, dx = \frac{\pi}{2}$$

and

```
$$a(\lambda) = {1 \over {2\pi}} \int\displaylimits
_{-\infty}^{+\infty} f(x)e^{-i\lambda x}\,dx$$
```

produces

$$a(\lambda) = \frac{1}{2\pi} \int\limits_{-\infty}^{+\infty} f(x)e^{-i\lambda x}\, dx$$

From (Abrahams, Berry, and Hargreaves, 1990)

Figure 3.3: Examples can be ordered based on complexity.

```
(aardvark)                        ; example of a list
'aardvark                         ; not a list

(1)                               ; example of a list
1                                 ; not a list

(blue sky)                        ; a list of atoms
(1 4 6 8 9)                       ; a list of numbers
(10 white clouds)                 ; a list of atoms
                                    and a number

((blue sky) (10 white clouds))    ; a list of lists
```
                                    From (Novak, 1985), p. 4.

Figure 3.4: Sequences carry implicit information in example sequences.

```
(blue sky)                        ; list of atoms
(10 white clouds)                 ; list of atoms
                                    and numbers
(1)                               ; a list
ardvark)                          ; another list
1                                 ; not a list
'aardvark                         ; not a list
(1 4 6 8 9)                       ; list of numbers
((blue sky) (10 white clouds))    ; list of lists
```

Figure 3.5: Bad sequencing can cause loss of information content.

examples, one positive (possessing the feature) and another negative (similar to the positive one, but *without* the critical feature). *Variable* features are best illustrated through a collection of positive examples similar to each other but varying widely in their variable features. To minimize information loss through bad sequencing (and to prevent the user from the errors of either overgeneralization or undergeneralization), the system should use the following two principles in structuring example presentations:

1. *Principle of Maximum Positive Variation:* There should be maximum possible variation between positive examples about the same feature — this prevents the hearer from undergeneralizing the concept based on the examples presented.

2. *Principle of Minimum Negative Difference:* There should be minimal difference between positive and negative examples about the same feature — this helps the hearer rule out the maximum possible number of noncritical features. Features that change between a positive and negative example are then easier to identify as critical features. If the two examples are minimally different, there will be fewer features to consider as possible critical candidates.

Because the examples are an integrated part of the accompanying description an additional constraint in the order of example presentation is often the order in which the various features are mentioned in the accompanying description, or vice versa.

Finally, possible example sequence orderings can also depend on factors such as the type of concept being communicated: whether it is a disjunctive or a conjunctive concept, and whether it is a relation or a process. In an interesting extension to the concept of sequencing, Tennyson and Tennyson (1975) found that an animated presentation where the positive example changed to a negative one, was more effective than the presentation of examples in a static sequence, because it drew attention to the differences between the two examples.

The significance of the order of presentation is particularly evident from a curious anomalous result on the theoretical limits of languages that can be learned from examples. Gold (1965, 1967) showed that certain concepts that could not be learned when both positive and negative examples are presented, could however be learnt solely from positive

An `assignment` is a construct that tells TeX to assign a value to a register, to an internal parameter, to an entry in an internal table, or to a control sequence. Some examples of assignments are:

```
\tolerance = 2000
\advance\count12 by 17
\lineskip4pt plus 2pt
\everycr = {\hskip 3pt relax}
\catcode\'@ = 11
\let\graf = \par
\font\myfont cmbx12
```

From (Abrahams, Berry, and Hargreaves, 1990), p. 49.

An `assignment` is a construct that tells TeX to assign a value to a register, to an internal parameter, to an entry in an internal table, or to a control sequence. *The variable being assigned a value is specified first on the left, followed by the value. The variable and the value can be optionally separated by the '=' character, or a space. The value can be either a number, a dimension with units, a variable name, an expression, a control character or a font name.*

Figure 3.6: Example of textual elision due to examples.

examples *when the presentation sequence was carefully constructed.* This is the class of recursively enumerable languages. Consider for example the class of Fibonacci numbers. Given a sequence such as **5, 1, 21, 8, 2, 3, 13**, the reader is unlikely to be able to recognize the concept. However, should the sequence be presented as **1, 2, 3, 5, 8, 13, 21**, there is a much better chance that the hearer will recognize the *sequence* and be able to generalize to the set of Fibonacci numbers. The hearer actually recognizes the generating function or the algorithm to generate the examples rather than the concept description itself. This illustrates the importance of sequencing examples carefully.

3.7   Positioning Examples With Respect to the Accompanying Description

Once an appropriate example has been generated, it needs to be presented with the accompanying explanation. Should the example be presented *before, within* or *after* the textual explanation? An example can either play a "supporting" role where it illustrates the preceding text, or it can be the focus or subject of the text. Depending on the role, the example either occurs *after* the definition of the concept, or *before* the description of concept, based on the example. If the text is introductory, the examples are used to illustrate each attribute of the concept, immediately following the presentation of the attribute in the definition. This results in descriptions where each attribute specification is followed by examples, resulting in a description with examples interspersed *within* it.

When examples are used to elaborate on points that are not explicitly mentioned in the textual description they are often interwoven with the textual description of the concept. They could have been replaced by text elaborating on these points. This was illustrated in the description of the TEX assignment operation, as shown in figure 1.2, repeated here for clarity, in figure 3.6. In this case, the examples could be replaced by a statement that conveys all the features being illustrated through examples, as shown in the lower half of the figure.

In another example, consider the description of a list given in figure 3.7.[6] The examples of list (in group II) of figure 3.7 communicate

---

[6]The text and examples have been delineated by us for clarity: the text is framed by

| I | A list always begins with a left parenthesis. Then come zero or more pieces of data   (called the elements of the list), and a right parenthesis. Some examples of lists are: |

| II | (AARDVARK)
(RED YELLOW GREEN BLUE)
(2 3 5 11 19)
(3 FRENCH FRIES) |

| III | A List may contain other lists as elements. ‖ Given the three lists: |

| IV | (BLUE SKY)   (GREEN GRASS)   (BROWN EARTH)
we can make a list by combining them all with a parenthesis:
((BLUE SKY) (GREEN GRASS) (BROWN EARTH)) |

From (Touretzky, 1984), p. 35.

Figure 3.7: A description of list using examples.

information that could have been expressed textually by the following sentence: *"The elements of the list can be either symbols, numbers, or a combination of these two."* In this case, the examples *replaced* the sentence above; however, the system may choose to elaborate using *both* examples, as well as text. This is illustrated by groups III and IV in the figure, in which the information about lists being made up of sublists is expressed both textually (in III) and then by means of an example (in IV). The choice between text and examples depends upon both the text type and the concept being illustrated. In the case of an introductory text, examples are presented if the definition has already been presented. In the case of anomalous or exceptional features, *both* the text and the examples are presented. This is illustrated in the list case, where sublists need to be presented. This is a recursive example, and the system presents it using both text and examples. This illustrates the point that examples cannot just be inserted in a dogmatic fashion at the end of a description.

The importance of the placement of examples is even greater when there are a large number of examples. Consider for instance, the description given in figure 3.8. The examples are provided at appropriate points *in* the description, rather being all placed at the end of the description. Although the equivalent description in figure 3.9 is possible, most introductory texts resemble the description in figure 3.8.

3.8   Prompt Generation for the Examples

Examples can communicate a lot of information, some of which is communicated through their ordering. However, this information can sometimes be lost on the reader, especially if he or she is unable to discern the critical difference between juxtaposed examples. To prevent this, one can attempt to draw the reader's attention to the salient point through the use of *prompts*. Prompts are symbols or additional information presented along with the examples to help focus the reader's attention on the critical attributes. Consider for instance the examples in figure 3.10. The notes in comments on the right represent prompts, focusing attention on a particular feature of the example. Prompts are often used to replace long, detailed explanations about the examples.

---

a clear box, while the examples appear in shaded boxes.

Numbers and symbols cannot be used as inputs to CAR because numbers and symbols, unlike lists, are not built of CONS cells. Taking the CAR of FROB, for example, causes an ERROR.

```
(CAR 'FROB) ==> Error! Not a list.
```

The function CDR returns the input list after removing its first element. Thus, for example:

```
(CDR '(FOO BAR BAZ)) ==> (BAR BAZ)
(CDR '(A B C D))      ==> (B C D)
```

The CDR of a single-element list is the empty list, NIL.

```
(CDR (FROB)) ==> NIL
```

CDR will not work on inputs that are not lists:

```
(CDR 'FROB) ==> Error! Not a list.
```

CAR and CDR work on nested lists just as easily as on flat ones. For example:

```
(CAR '((BLUE CUBE) (RED PYRAMID))) ==> (BLUE CUBE)
(CDR '((BLUE CUBE) (RED PYRAMID))) ==> (RED PYRAMID)
```

Two more pairs are:

```
(CAR '((A B) (C D) (E F))) ==> (A B)
(CDR '((A B) (C D) (E F))) ==> ((C D) (E F))
```

From (Winston and Horn, 1984), p. 24.

Figure 3.8: A description with a large number of examples of the functions CAR and CDR.

The function CDR returns the input list after removing its first element. The CDR of a single-element list is the empty list, NIL. CDR will not work on inputs that are not lists. CAR and CDR work on nested lists just as easily as on flat ones. For example:

```
(CDR '(FOO BAR BAZ)) ==> (BAR BAZ)
(CDR (FROB)) ==> NIL
(CDR 'FROB) ==> Error! Not a list.
(CAR '((A B) (C D) (E F))) ==> (A B)
(CDR '((A B) (C D) (E F))) ==> ((C D) (E F))
```

Figure 3.9: Alternative description for the functions CAR and CDR.

Carnine (1980) demonstrated that drawing attention to the changing attributes can significantly help the user focus on critical features of the examples and enhance understandability. There are many ways in which prompts can be generated. For instance, the critical features could have been indicated using **bold** or *italic* typefaces. An example of this is illustrated in figure 3.11. The writer is describing the use of the **moveto** operator, and presents a small code fragment in which it appears. To highlight the statement, the rest of the code is shown in grey (in the actual book), while the statement being considered is shown in bold face. In this work, we only consider the case of textual prompts like the ones shown in figure 3.10.

3.9   Summary

The term *example* derives from the 14th century Latin term *exemplum*, which meant "a clearing in the woods" (Webster, 1997). Exemplum, in turn, is also related to to the verb *exi-mere, "to take out, to remove, to take away, to free, to make an exception of."* In this sense, example is synonymous with a more contemporary term: *detail*. The detail is also removed, cut out (*dé* + *tailler* in French). In origin and usage, an example, as a "clearing in the woods," suggests the sense of the term as

The **idleArry** contains the information used by postscript for idle time
font scan conversion. The array can be broken down into groups containing different pieces of information. For example:

```
/Times-Bold                          % font name
14                                   % x scale
14                                   % y scale
0                                    % rotation
                                     % conversion characters
(abcdefghijklmnopqrstuvwxyz)         % string length = 26
```

From (Braswell, 1989), p. 8–5.

A function to convert temperatures from Fahrenheit to Celsius could
be written as:

```
(DEFUN F-TO-C (TEMP)
    (SETQ TEMP (- TEMP 32))          ; Subtract
    (/ TEMP 1.8)))                   ; Divide
```

From (Winston and Horn, 1984), p. 43.

Examples of control strings are:

"~S"	;	*An ~S directive with no parameters or modifiers*
"~3,-4:@s"	;	*An ~S directive with two parameters, 3 and -4,*
	;	*and both the colon and at-sign flags*
"~,+4S"	;	*First prefix parameter is omitted and takes*
	;	*on its default value; the second parameter is 4*

From (Steele Jr., 1984), p. 386.

Figure 3.10: Prompts are often used in examples.

Consider the code to draw a triangle given below. The second line of the program is the first real line of code — an instruction to position the pen on the page. **72 144 moveto** is an instruction to move to position (72, 144) on the page.

```
%!PS                % Postscript magic number
72 144 moveto       % set initial point
306 648 lineto      % add line segment
540 144 lineto      % add another line segment
closepath           % finish the shape
stroke              % paint the path
showpage            % display page
```

From (McGilton and Campione, 1992), p. 11.

Figure 3.11: A typeface change can be an effective prompt.

a rhetorical figure that gives form or boundary to the surrounding argument and provides specific details to a much more general definition or discussion, while its very existence as an effective rhetorical device depends upon its surrounding argument; there would be no clearing without a wood to surround it; an example would not be one without accompanying discourse to define it.

This chapter has discussed some of the basic issues that arise in the presentation of descriptions that integrate both textual descriptions and examples. These issues were identified from our corpus of programming language manuals and text books. Although some of these may be more relevant to software documentation than to other domains (such as physical devices, for instance), they are, nevertheless, important, and need to be considered by any generation system.

One issue that also arises in the integration of text and examples is the choice of lexical items for the text and the examples. Empirical work on lexical choice includes studies by Feldman and Klausmeier (1974) on the effect of different lexical terms in the definitions and the examples. Their study demonstrated that confusion and ambiguity was minimized by a consistent choice of the lexical terms, in both the definition and the example. Another study by Ward and Sweller

(1990), showed that instructional and explanatory materials were most effective when they presented the definitions and the examples using the same lexical terms and constructions. It is therefore important to ensure that the lexical items used in both the descriptions and the examples be used consistently. However, the issue of lexical choice is a complicated one, and currently outside the scope of this work. In our system implementation, since both the text and the examples are generated using the same planner, we ensure that the terms used in both the text and the examples are consistent.

In the following chapter, we describe a scheme for categorizing example types, one that differs significantly from all previously proposed categorizations. This categorization enables us to find appropriate examples in different situations, and use previous results from educational psychology on good presentation sequences for examples illustrating concepts belonging to certain categories. The chapters following that will be concerned with the actual system implementation, and present different traces of the system as it generates different scenarios.

Chapter 4

A Categorization of Example Types

The previous chapter discussed a number of issues related to the presentation of examples as part of integrated descriptions. Some of the issues raised there used the terms 'positive' and 'negative' examples. Are there any other types of examples? What are they, and how are they characterized? In this chapter, we consider these questions. We categorize examples into different classes and define them.

4.1 The Need for Categorizing Examples

Since examples play an important role in comprehension (Houtz, Moore, and Davis, 1973; Pirolli, 1991; Reder, Charney, and Morgan, 1986), it is important for a system to be able to present examples to the user. A large number of examples can potentially be used to illustrate a given point. However, not all examples are equally effective in all situations; some are better than others in specific contexts, and others tend to illustrate different aspects of the same concept in different ways and achieve different goals. Categorizing examples is useful because identifying a category to generate an example from can greatly constrain the number of possible examples that can be applicable in the given situation.

Previous studies on the categorization of examples include studies by Polya (1945) and Michener (1978) on the suitability of examples in different situations. However, these categorizations did not explicitly take into account the *context* in which the example was presented. Yet, the context of an example affects its characterization and usefulness. To use examples effectively — as an important and a complementary part of the overall description — the system must reason with the constraints introduced by both the textual explanation, as well as the examples. This is because both the *examples and the surrounding description affect each other*.

This chapter discusses the issue of characterizing the *type of examples* that appear in natural language descriptions. This can be of great help to a system in choosing appropriate examples to present. We first describe previous work on categorizing example types, and illustrate how the same example can be categorized in two different categories if the accompanying description is not taken into account. Then, we present a new categorization that takes the context into consideration. This categorization is based on three orthogonal dimensions: (a) the *information content*, (b) the *text type*, and (c) the *knowledge type* of the example.

4.2   Categorizing Examples: Previous Work

Polya (1945) categorized examples into three categories:

1. leading examples

2. suggestive examples

3. counter examples

Leading examples were ones that contained mostly *critical*[1] features and very few *variable*[2] features; they were meant for naive users. Sug-

---

[1]As discussed in chapter 3, critical features are features that are necessary for an example to be considered a positive example of a concept. Changes to a critical feature cause a positive example to become a negative example.

[2]Variable features are features that can *vary* in a positive example. Changes to variable features create different positive examples.

gestive examples contained more variable features than leading examples and were meant to guide the student in the correct direction. Counter-examples were negative examples that illustrated how instances were *not* indicative of some concept.

In her work, Michener categorized examples into five categories (Michener 1977; 1978):

1. *introductory examples:* perspicuous, simple cases,

2. *model examples:* general, paradigmatic cases,

3. *reference examples:* standard, ubiquitous cases,

4. *counter examples:* limiting, falsifying cases, and

5. *anomalous examples:* exceptional, pathological cases.

These categorizations make significant contributions to our understanding, but are deficient in two respects:

1. because they do not explicitly take into account the context of the presentation, the same example can often be classified into different categories;

2. the definition of the category is not clearly specified; it is therefore difficult to implement in a computational system.

Furthermore, the two categorizations above did not specify relationships (if any) between their different categories, nor did they specify whether these categories were mutually exclusive.

4.3 Categorizing Examples in Context

Our categorization of examples was driven by the need to be able to generate tutorial and explanatory descriptions that integrate text and examples coherently in a computational framework. In such a framework, a system must be able to present suitable examples to illustrate the description or the definition being presented. The suitability of an example is determined *in the context it appears in, rather than in the abstract*: it depends upon the goal of the description, what features are being presented, where in the overall description the example appears, etc.

Furthermore, the suitability of the example is also affected by other examples around it. As we have described in section 3.6, the presentation order of the examples plays an important role in reader comprehension. Thus, the appropriateness of a single example, presented for the same description, can be different based on other examples that appear with it, and where in the presentation sequence it appears. It would therefore seem obvious that an example can be categorized only in conjunction with the context in which it appears.

We now describe the three dimensions that characterize an example in context: (1) the relationship of the information in the example to that in the context; (2) the text type in which the example is to be generated within; and (3) the knowledge type being communicated by the examples.

4.3.1   The First Dimension: The Relationship of the Example to the Description

One of the dimensions that an example can be characterized along is the relationship of the information contained in the example with the information contained in the accompanying descriptive explanation that it illustrates. Along this dimension, an example can fall into three categories:

Positive Examples: These examples are instances of the concept being described and satisfy the properties of the concept as described in the accompanying description. These examples must possess all the critical features of the concept they illustrate. Such examples are usually in an *elaborative* role to the information in the description.

Negative Examples: Negative examples (or counter-examples) are *not* instances of the concept being described. These are cases that *do not* meet the requirements specified in the accompanying description, and they play a *contrastive* role in the context.

Negative examples can be very useful because they help rule out non-critical features of a concept (Houtz, Moore, and Davis, 1973). For in-

---

(AARDVARK)	; example of a list
AARDVARK	; not a list

Figure 4.1: Two examples about a list.

---

stance, the examples of a list in the programming language LISP in figure 4.1 illustrate the need for parentheses in a list. The negative example conveys the information that the symbol AARDVARK by itself is not sufficient for an instance to be a list. By virtue of the fact that the only difference between a positive and a negative example is the set of parentheses, it draws attention to the fact that the parentheses are important for something to be a list. Thus, *features in common* between positive and negative examples *can be ruled out as sufficient* features, while *differing features* are highlighted as *necessary* features and thus become more important.

Anomalous Examples: Anomalous examples represent irregular or exceptional cases. These are either: (a) instances of the concept described, but not covered by the description, or (b) instances likely to be misclassified by the reader (because of an incomplete description). Thus, positive instances which appear to be very different from other positive examples, or negative instances which appear to be very similar to positive examples, would be classified as anomalous cases. Anomalous examples must be presented with appropriate introductory text, and presented apart from the other examples (Engelmann and Carnine, 1982).

The classification of an example into either of these categories depends on the context established by the accompanying descriptive explanation. For instance, an anomalous example in one context could classified as a normal, positive example in another context. Consider the following description of a list in LISP:

A left parenthesis, followed by zero or more S-expressions, followed by a right parenthesis is a list.

From (Shapiro, 1986)

Given the above definition of a list, the following examples would classify as positive, negative, and anomalous cases:

Positive Examples	Negative Examples	Anomalous
(A B C D)	'ATOM	NIL
(1 2 3 4 5 67)	1234567	
(BLUE SKIES GREEN GRASS)	'BLUE	

This categorization of examples could change with another definition:

> A list is a CONS-cell whose CDR is either the atom NIL or another list. The atom NIL is the identifier that represents the empty list and the boolean concept FALSE.

From (Steele Jr., 1984)

In this case, NIL *becomes a positive example* of a list. Similarly, a list may be so defined as to include the concept of a dotted-list as well.

It is clear that it is difficult, and sometimes impossible, to classify an example as belonging to a certain category without taking into consideration the surrounding contextual information. It is also difficult to categorize examples as being "suggestive," "model" or "reference" without having a complete definition of these different categories. Correct classification of the examples is essential, because examples must be presented in accordance with the category they happen to classify in. For instance, anomalous examples need to be presented separately from the regular examples, with a suitable introduction to notify the user of the anomalous nature of such examples.

4.3.2   The Second Dimension: The Text Type

The second dimension that examples can be characterized along is dictated by the text type in which the generation is to take place. It has long been observed that naturally occurring texts fall into certain linguistic patterns which characterize the genre of that text. Many of these genres, such as scientific papers and financial reports (among others) impose strong constraints on both the type and frequency of occurrence for certain types of linguistic phenomena such as the rhetorical structure, lexical types, grammatical features, etc. (Hovy et al., 1992). Several text typologies have been proposed by linguists over the years; Biber (1988, 1989) identified eight basic types of texts based on statistically derived grammatical and lexical commonalities; de Beaugrande (1980) proposed another general classification of text types, arguing, in addition, that text types determine the types of discourse structure relations used.

The text type is an important constraint on the selection of information to be presented *both* in the description and the example. In our case, we only use three different text types in our categorization: (a) introductory texts, (b) intermediate texts, and (c) advanced, or reference manual type texts. Since these text types are based on the intended user,[3] results in user modelling can also be taken into account. Among the many studies on the need for varying both the amount of information and the manner of presentation based on the user are (Paris, 1993; Paris, 1988; Nwana, 1991; London, 1992). The results from these studies, on the differences in the textual descriptions presented to the user should also be taken into account.

As we have already mentioned before, the major shortcoming of both previous example categorizations was due to the fact that they did not take the accompanying context into account. In contrast, we consider *both* the description and the example for categorization. This is essential, because our system needs to generate both the text as well as the example in its explanation.

From our corpus analyses, we have classified examples in the context of their accompanying descriptions into three main classes — *introductory*, *intermediate* and *advanced*. This classification constrains both the content and the presentation style of the descriptions and the examples:

1. *introductory:* text type meant for users with little or no previous exposure assumed for the concept; goal is *to learn about* the concept,

2. *intermediate:* text type meant for users with moderate previous

---

[3]There is a close correspondence between the text type and the intended user type. Thus, this dimension can also be labelled as the intended user type.

exposure; goal is *to learn to make use* of the concept,

3. *advanced:* text type meant for users with extensive knowledge; goal is *to clarify some point or misconception* about the concept.

Introductory Texts: Examples in introductory descriptions tend to be simple ones — where 'simple' refers to the fact that they are usually single-featured (or if they have multiple features, usually no more than two, where the two features are along two different feature dimensions). This has also been reported in other studies (Clark, 1971; Michener, 1977; Carnine, 1980b; Litchfield, Driscoll, and Dempsey, 1990). In our domain of programming languages, the accompanying description is syntactic or surface-appearance oriented. Anomalous examples are usually absent, and if they are presented, they only appear *after* all the other examples. Examples are often introduced as soon as the point they illustrate is mentioned in the text.

Consider for instance the description in figure 4.2. The descriptions are centered around the syntax or the surface appearance of the `list`. The examples are simple and illustrate one feature at a time (the *type* of data elements, except in one case where the *type* and the *number*, two different dimensions of variation, are illustrated). Examples do not always have prompts, because the same information is usually realized as sentences in the accompanying description.

Intermediate Texts: Descriptions written for the 'intermediate' reader (who is already assumed to have introductory knowledge) tend to be more complex than the ones for introductory users, in that they include more detail on *how* the information may be *used* by the user. The examples are not always presented immediately; if there are a number of related points, these points are stated first, before a group of examples illustrating these points are presented. The examples themselves are usually briefly annotated (with prompts). Intermediate descriptions contain a few introductory examples, that are then followed by examples that illustrate the use of the concept. For example, the description in figure 4.3 describes how a `list` can be used to represent shopping lists, store phone numbers, and write function calls.

Reference or Advanced Texts: Since the purpose of advanced or reference materials is *not* instruction, it is not surprising that both the

A list always begins with a left parenthesis. Then come zero or more pieces of data (called the elements of a list) and a right parenthesis. Some examples of lists are:

```
(AARDVARK)
(RED YELLOW GREEN BLUE)
(2 3 5 11 19)
(3 FRENCH FRIES)
```

A list may contain other lists as elements. Given the three lists:

```
(BLUE SKY)
(GREEN GRASS)
(BROWN EARTH)
```

we can make a list by combining them all with parentheses.

```
((BLUE SKY) (GREEN GRASS) (BROWN EARTH))
```

From (Touretzky, 1984), p. 35.

Figure 4.2: Introductory examples are usually single featured.

A list looks like a sequence of objects, without commas between them, enclosed in parentheses.

    ⋮

Appropriately constructed lists can also be used to call functions in LISP. If you type any of the lists in table 2–4 to LISP, you will get an appropriate response.

Table 2-2:
```
(1 2 3 4 5)                              ; a list of numbers
(A B C D)                               ; a list of symbols
(#\A #\B #\C #\D)                       ; list of characters
```

Table 2-3:
```
(This is (also) a list)                 ; third element is also a list
((12 eggs (large))
 (1 bread (whole wheat))
 (4 pizzas (frozen with anchovies)))    ; list of lists of numbers,
                                        ; symbols and lists
("this is a string in a list" -53)     ; list of a string and a
                                        ; number
((Beth "555-5834") (Pat "555-8098"))   ; list containing
                                        ; two lists
```

Table 2-4:
```
(SQRT 2)             ; the first element is the name of a function
(+ 2 3)              ; the first element is the name of a function
(- 6 5 4)            ; the first element is the name of a function
```

Lists can be considered ways to store data. For example, you might want to store your inventory as a list, or group together names and phone numbers in a list.

From (Tatar, 1987), p. 16.

Figure 4.3: Intermediate 'use' oriented examples.

A list is recursively defined to be either the empty list or a CONS whose CDR component is a list. The CAR components of the CONSes are called the elements of the list. For each element of the list, there is a CONS. The empty list has no elements at all.

A list is annotated by writing the elements of the list in order, separated by blank space (space, tab, or return character) and surrounded by parentheses. For example:

```
(a b c)                 ;  a list of 3 symbols
(2.0s0 (a 1) #\*)       ;  a list of 3 things:
                        ;    a floating point number,
                        ;    another list, and a
                        ;    character object
```

The empty list NIL therefore can be written ( ), because it is a list with no elements.

From (Steele Jr., 1984), p. 26.

Figure 4.4: Reference manuals have fewer, more complex examples.

textual description and the accompanying examples are very different from those in the introductory ones. The documentation and the examples usually occur in a fixed format, with the examples following the definition and the explanation. The examples are not simple, single-featured, but tend to be few and multi-featured. The examples are often almost independent of the textual description, with little cross-referencing between the two. This almost invariably results in prompts being used to indicate some of the salient characteristics of the examples. Because the descriptions tend to be comprehensive, there are few (if any) anomalous examples. If there are any anomalous examples, they are always presented. For example, a description of a list from an advanced, reference manual is shown in figure 4.4.

4.3.3   The Third Dimension: The Knowledge Type

The *knowledge type* can also be used during the generation process to determine the appropriate type and sequence of examples to be generated in an explanation. The *knowledge type* refers to the categorization of information into one of three broad classes: *concepts*, *relations*, or *processes*. There can be significant differences in the presentation of examples and the accompanying descriptions based on whether the idea to be explained is a concept, a relation or a process. Consider for instance the *concept* 'list' (as described in figure 4.2) and the *relation* 'list' (functions are relations that hold between the input parameters and the output values of the function), as illustrated in figure 4.5.

The *concept* list is described as an object, and examples of list are instances of this object; the *function* list, on the other hand, is described in terms of its input and output parameters, and examples of the function reflect this fact. Similarly, *processes*, which are sequences of functions, are described differently and their examples are often instances of function parameters at every step in the sequence. In generating examples of relations, it is important to keep in consideration that the examples used as input-output parameters must be known to the hearer. Also, since anomalous or pathological examples of concepts used as either input or output examples for examples of relations often result in anomalous examples of relations, the examples must be chosen carefully.

Examples of processes consist of chains of events that take place in

The `list` function takes any number of inputs and makes a list of them all. For example:

INPUT to `list`		OUTPUT
foo bar baz	→	(foo bar baz)
foo	→	(foo)
(frob)	→	((frob))

From (Touretzky, 1984), p. 51

Figure 4.5: Examples of a relation.

a particular order. The goal is to communicate the *sequence of events* and their *cumulative effect*. In case the reader does not know about certain relations or concepts involved in the steps of the routine, the generator must adequately explain such relations or concepts as well. This is to ensure that the hearer is familiar with the rest of the steps in the sequence before the difficult examples are encountered.

4.4 Discussion

In this chapter, we have presented one method of categorizing example types. Such a categorization is important, because different situations often require the presentation of different types of examples with specific presentation requirements about the number of examples, the sequence of presentation, the associated prompts, and so on (Engelmann and Carnine, 1982). A specification of the different presentation requirements is particularly important in designing an effective explanation system. We have argued that examples must be characterized based on the context where they appear. We have presented one such characterization, and illustrated it with examples from our corpus.

Our categorization is a generalization of the previous work by Michener and Polya, and extends the scope of the characterization to take

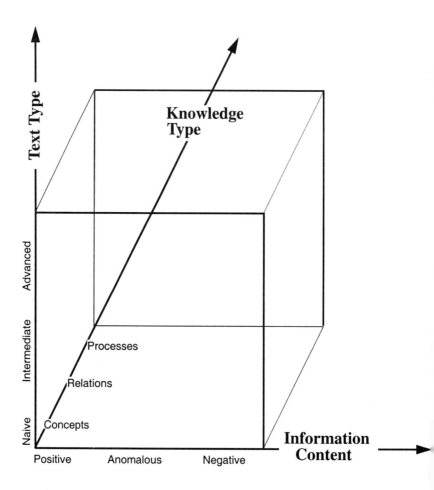

Figure 4.6: The three dimensions used in categorization.

into account the surrounding context of the example. This is important in generating well integrated text and examples. The categories along each of the three dimensions that we have mentioned can be subdivided further into smaller classes, and specific presentation methods can be associated with each class.[4]

This categorization is not specific to a particular architecture for generation, and can be easily incorporated into any system such as CEG (Suthers and Rissland, 1988) or HYPO (Ashley, 1991). The dimensions can be further refined or modified if necessary to suit particular applications: for instance, recent work on categorizing *dialectical examples* (Ashley and Aleven, 1992) can be easily incorporated into our framework by further dividing the positive example category into "representational," "conflict resolution," "ceteris paribus" and "coherence" categories.[5] Our categorization is general in the sense that it does not depend upon the aspect an example is supposed to illustrate. Given a particular context in a particular application domain, our classification scheme can be further refined into many different sub-categories. In addition, this categorization can help a system partition the search in the example knowledge base for suitable examples. Given that a particular concept needs to be illustrated, the system need only consider examples that meet the classification criteria, for instance, positive, simple (introductory texts) of a concept.

The following chapter describes an implemented system to generate integrated descriptions.

---

[4]Some of these issues were discussed in classical rhetoric as well, with Erasmus (1979) discussing the need for both context and the variety of goals that can be fulfilled by the same example ("many purposes the same illustrative example can serve").

[5]These categories are all defined as positive examples, with different characteristics, depending upon the feature(s) they illustrate in the context of legal reasoning.

Chapter 5

The System Implementation

In the previous chapters, we have presented the motivation, related work, relevant issues, and a categorization of different example types. In this chapter, we describe an implementation of a system capable of generating descriptions with integrated text and examples. The system consists of four major components: the text planner, the example generator, the knowledge representation, and the English interface (the grammar interface and the sentence realizer). As the basis for our implementation, we use the EES text planning system (Moore and Paris, 1989; Moore and Paris, 1988; Moore, 1995), to which we have added an example generator that retrieves and constructs actual examples given a specification of what is required. The planning system has access to several knowledge sources, such as the domain knowledge, the user model and the dialogue history containing a record of the previous discourse. While planning, the system passes requests for examples to the example generator. The output of the planning phase is a discourse structure tree, which is then passed through an interface and a sentence generator to produce English. A block diagram of the overall architecture is shown in figure 5.1.

The rest of this chapter describes the text planner, the knowledge representation, and the example generator in more detail.

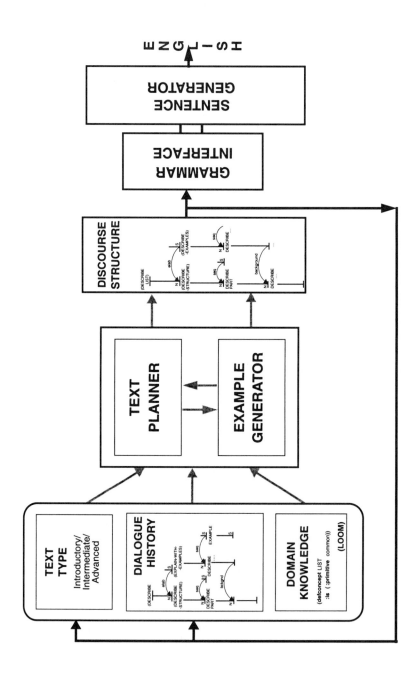

Figure 5.1: A block diagram of the overall system.

5.1 The Text Planner

The system uses a text planning framework to plan the overall discourse in terms of high level communicative goals. It uses a hierarachical, linear planning mechanism — based on the STRIPS planner (Fikes and Nilsson, 1990) — to plan the structure of the discourse: given a top level communicative goal, the system finds plans capable of achieving this goal. Plans typically post further subgoals to be satisfied, and planning continues until primitive speech acts — directly realizable in English — are achieved. The result of the planning process is a discourse tree, where the nodes represent goals at various levels of abstraction with the root being the initial goal, and the leaves representing primitive realization statements, such as (INFORM ...) statements.

To ensure that the generated text is coherent, the system selects plan operators such that each communicative goal in the discourse tree is related to adjacent communicative goals through *coherence relations*. Coherence relations are used to generate appropriate connectives during the realization phase. We use relations from Rhetorical Structure Theory (RST) (Mann and Thompson, 1988) as our set of coherence relations.

The resulting discourse tree is then passed to a grammar interface which converts it into a set of inputs suitable for input to a sentence generator, which results in the actual English output. A detailed description of the system can be seen in (Moore, 1995; Moore and Paris, 1989; Paris, 1991; Moore and Paris, 1991; Moore and Paris, 1992).

5.1.1 Plan Operators

Plan operators describe how to achieve a communicative goal. They are designed by studying (large) corpora of natural language texts and transcripts. They include conditions for their applicability. These conditions can refer to resources like the system knowledge base (KB), the user model, or the context (i.e., the dialogue context, the current text being generated, the text type, etc.). A sample text plan operator is shown in figure 5.2. The operator has four slots:

EFFECT: a specification of the goals that the plan operator may be capable of achieving; in the case of the plan operator in figure 5.2,

```
(define-text-plan-operator
  :EFFECT (elaboration-by-example ?ftr ?object)
  :CONSTRAINTS
       (and
         (isa? ?object concept)
         (get-example-available ?example ?ftr ?object)
         (prompt-required? ?example ?ftr ?object))
  :NUCLEUS (present-example ?example)
  :SATELLITES (elaboration
                    (example-prompt ?ftr ?object))))
```

Figure 5.2: Sample Text Plan Operator.

the EFFECT specifies that the operator can achieve the goal of presenting an example of an object (the variable ?object) to illustrate a particular feature (the variable ?ftr).

CONSTRAINTS: the preconditions that must be true in the environment for the operator to be selected. These constraints can be either predicates or functions that bind variables to specific values. For instance, in the case of figure 5.2, the constraints check: (a) whether the object being described is a *concept* (as opposed to a relation, or a process, for instance); (b) whether an example is available (can either be retrieved or constructed) to illustrate the feature ?ftr in the object ?object — this will cause the generation of the actual example, and if successful, bind it to the variable ?example; if there is no example that can be either found or constructed, this constraint will fail, causing this plan operator to not be selected; (c) whether a prompt is required for the example selected (?example) for the object (?object) for feature (?ftr). Of the three constraints, the first and the third constraints are purely predicate in nature, while the second one actually binds a variable with a new value.

NUCLEUS and SATELLITE: according to RST, the communicative goal specified in the EFFECT slot can be achieved by providing some information. This information can often be further partitioned into two parts: (a) information playing the *central* role, which must necessarily be communicated: this is represented by the goals in the NUCLEUS; (b) information playing a supportive role; such information is often used as background material, or as elaboration upon the information in the NUCLEUS: this is represented by the goals in the SATELLITE position. Information in the SATELLITE is often not *required* for the original discourse goal to be satisfied; in such cases, the SATELLITE may be marked '*optional*.' As stated earlier, the sibling goals posted as a result of the NUCLEUS and SATELLITE subgoals must be related through the use of coherence relations: in this case, the relation 'elaboration' marks the relationship of the information in the SATELLITE to that in the NUCLEUS.

In this framework, experimenting with additional sources of knowledge in the planner is not difficult, because these additional sources can be added to the system by incorporating additional constraints in the plan operators which reference these resources. In this system examples are generated by explicitly posting a goal within the text planning system: i.e., some of the plan operators used in the system include the generation of examples as one of their steps, when applicable. (figure 5.2 shows a sample plan operator that can be used to present examples.) This ensures that the examples embody specific information that either illustrates or complements the information in the accompanying textual description. A snapshot of the screen with the text planner is shown in figure 5.3. This shows the discourse structure being constructed, the plan operator being evaluated by the system at that time, and another window with a trace containing information on constraints being tested.

At present, the system has about 60 plan operators in our domain of software documentation that deal with the generation of concept descriptions with examples.

5.2 The Knowledge Representation

Our system is part of the documentation facility we are building for the **Explainable Expert Systems** (EES) Project (Swartout, Paris, and

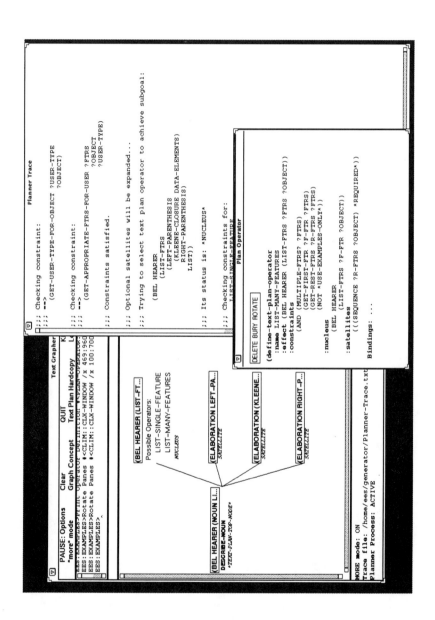

Figure 5.3: A snapshot of the system interface.

```
action-role-form :=
    '( action-role-name restricted-expression ') ;

predicate-form :=
    pred-value-form   |   pred-relation-form   |
    pred-logical-form  |   pred-action-form  || ;

pred-relation-form :=
    '( relation-description restricted-expression + ')
      |> predicate-relation-form-test ;
```

Figure 5.4: A fragment of the EES grammar.

Moore, 1992), a framework for building expert systems capable of explaining their reasoning as well as their domain knowledge. In EES, a user specifies a domain model in the high level knowledge representation language LOOM (MacGregor, 1988),[1] as well as problem solving principles, that is, methods for solving problems in the domain. Given these and a variabilized goal to achieve, EES generates an expert system to solve goals of the same form.

The problem-solving methods have to be written in a specific plan language, INTEND, which was designed specifically for the project, with the goal of facilitating explanations. INTEND is specified in the Backus-Naur Form (BNF), a fragment of which is shown in figure 5.4. The grammar contains productions, and, optionally "filter functions" on the productions, that is, tests that have to be satisfied before the production can be selected. For instance, 'pred-relation-form-test' is a filter-function defined on the pred-relation-form production. The grammar of INTEND is quite complex, and thus provides a good testbed for a documentation facility. With such an online facility, users can get information as to what might be wrong when a plan does not parse, as well as descriptions of the various constructs involved, together with examples.

---

[1]Loom is a KL-ONE type language.

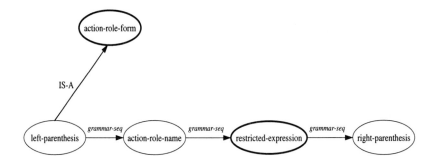

```
( defconcept ACTION-ROLE-FORM
  :is (:and left-parenthesis
       (:the grammar-sequence
             (:and action-role-name
                   (:the grammar-sequence
                         (:and RESTRICTED-EXPRESSION
                               (:the grammar-sequence right-parenthesis)))))))
```

Figure 5.5: Representing BNF productions in LOOM (thicker ovals in the diagram indicate non-terminals in the grammar).

To generate documentation, the system must first convert the BNF representation of the grammar to an equivalent LOOM representation. In our system, the BNF grammar is specified using POPART (Wile, 1987). The POPART representation of the BNF form can be easily converted (in most cases) to the desired LOOM representation.

The BNF representation must first be converted to LOOM for use by the generation facility; the form

```
A := B C;
```

is represented in LOOM as:

(defconcept A
  :is **(:and** B **(:the** grammar-sequence C)))

that is, concept A consists of concept B followed by (related by the relation named grammar-sequence to) concept C; the form

```
A := B | C;
```

is represented as a disjoint covering (B or C) under concept A.

(defconcept A
  :disjoint-covering (B C))

Consider also the production rules in the grammar shown in figure 5.4. The first production rule specifies that an action-role-form is an action-role-name followed by a restricted-expression, with both of these enclosed by parentheses. This is represented in LOOM as shown in figure 5.5. 'grammar-seq' is a relation defined to order the grammar symbols in the correct sequence. The non-terminal 'predicate-form' can be easily represented in LOOM as a disjunction of the four possibilities.

The production for a pred-relation-form is one that cannot be completely represented in LOOM automatically. This is due to the fact that the specification of a pred-relation-form is more than just the syntactic specification of restricted-expressions following a relation-description; the POPART representation also specifies that the form must satisfy the test represented by the filter function:

```
predicate-relation-form-test
```

These tests are defined in POPART to enforce non-syntactic constraints. For instance, in this case, the `predicate-relation-form-test` checks to see whether the number of `restricted-expressions` in the parse tree is equal to the arity of the `relation-description`. This is specified in the form of LISP code, and is currently manually transcribed into the LOOM definition of the concept. These BNF-to-LOOM transformations will be explained with the use of an example when we see how the system represents a `list`, in chapter 6.

There are many advantages to using a representation such as LOOM; the main one is the availability of the classifier mechanism. As we describe in the following section, the classifier allows the generation system to do two tasks very easily: (a) to categorize different features in an example as being either critical or variable, and (b) to determine if a negative example generated by the system is "interesting" or not.

5.3 The Example Generator

This section deals with the generation of examples to be used in the presentation. As discussed in section 5.1, the text planner posts explicit goals to present examples as part of the overall description. In this section, we discuss issues such as the construction, storage and retrieval of examples, the determination of their critical and variable features and whether prompts are required.

5.3.1 Construction of Examples

Examples can either be retrieved from a pre-existing Example Knowledge Base, as in HYPO (Ashley, 1991), or can be constructed, as in CEG (Suthers and Rissland, 1988).[2] Our system uses both *construction* and *retrieval* to find suitable examples. Initially, the system possesses examples of the primitive grammar elements such as atoms, numbers

---

[2]Aristotle discusses similar issues in his *Rhetoric*: examples that consist of things in the past, and examples that are invented in support of an argument. He discusses how examples, when they have not been made up on the spot, must be corrected in order to fit the current situation (Aristotle, 1926). Such modifications include "additions" or intensification (Aristotle, 1967), (as translated in (Weinberg, 1961), p. 523).

and strings in the LISP domain. Examples of such elements are therefore always retrieved. When the system needs to present an example of a more complex grammar symbol, such as a list, the system constructs the example based on the BNF definition of a list, as well as the features being illustrated. Unlike HYPO, which used 12 pre-defined features as indices, our system uses LOOM to allow us to retrieve examples with as few, or as many indices as necessary; the greater the number of indices specified in the retrieve, the fewer the number of possibilities returned by LOOM for consideration.

The example generator takes as input the list of features for a concept that needs to be illustrated by presenting an example of a particular object. The syntactic specification of the function and a typical call to it are given below:[3]

> **function:** get-example
> (get-example ?concept ?features ?object)
>
> **typical call:**
> (get-example 'data-element '(atom number) 'list)

In the function shown above, ?concept refers to the concept being illustrated, ?features specify the features of the concept that the example should try and illustrate, and ?object is the object whose example should be presented. Thus, in the instantiated function call shown here, the system constructs an example *of a list*, where the concept to be illustrated is that of *a data element*, and the features that need to be highlighted are the facts that a data element can be either an *atom or a number*. The resulting output from such a function call would be:

> (oranges 5)

The function accesses global constraints such as the text type to determine the type of elements required; in the case of the advanced text type, the element representing the number could have been a more complex, floating point number (this is done by specifying default types for the text type: lacking any further information, if a number is required for use in an example in an advanced text, the system will re-

---

[3]In the actual implementation, the function takes other arguments as well; these are to do with the variable that needs to be instantiated with the example, and so forth.

trieve a floating point number, as opposed to an integer.

The function `get-example` also takes an optional parameter, the `kl-clnumber`, which represents the number of elements desired for the feature in the concept that happens to be defined as a *kleene-closure*. In the case of a `list`, for instance, the BNF definition (in POPART notation) is:

```
list := `(  data-elements  *   `);
```

Because the default value of the `kl-clnumber` is one, if the parameter is not specified, the system will generate examples of lists with one `data-element` if no other information is available. In cases such as the one above, where the features to be exemplified are specified (in the variable `features`), the system will generate examples taking both the `kl-clnumber` and the features into account. The generated examples are then also stored in the knowledge base.

If the system is successful in generating an appropriate example, that example is then stored in LOOM as an example for the concept. Given the classification facility in LOOM, this is automatically indexed underneath a `list`, as well as any other grammar symbols it is applicable to. The next time the system needs to generate an example for the same features, the system can retrieve this example, rather than constructing one from scratch.

The function `get-example`, described here, is a relatively low-level function, in that it takes a very specific request for the object, as well as the features that need to be highlighted. This was done so as to make the text plan operators more explicit. The reasoning to determine the number and order of examples to be presented, determining the critical and variable features, and so on, is represented clearly in different constraints on the plan operators and are the focus of this study. This allows for easy modification of different strategies to observe their effects on the plan generated.

The next few subsections describe how the example generation component determines the critical and variable features, generates "interesting" negative examples and, if necessary, prompts, for the examples.

5.3.2 Determining Critical Features

As we mentioned earlier, in section 3.6, it is essential to convey to the user that some of the concept features are *required* for any instance to be an example of the concept. These features are referred to as *critical* features. To be able to emphasize the critical nature of a feature, the system can (in tutorial contexts), present a pair of examples, one positive and one negative, identical in all respects except for the critical feature being emphasized. To be able to do so, the system must be able to determine those features of the concept that are critical, and those that are not.[4]

In our system, the representation of the domain model in LOOM allows us to determine critical features relatively easily. This is because the classification facility in LOOM allows the system to query it regarding relationships between concepts and instances. This allows the system to determine whether a particular feature is critical or not, by simply modifying the value of each feature along various dimensions and then testing (querying LOOM) to see if the modified instance still classifies as an instance of the original object. We have defined for our domain a number of ways to modify the definition of a concept.[5] The system successively attempts these operators on the given concept definition, and finds those features whose modification causes the example to fail to classify under the object being explained. The modifications attempted by the system are given in figure 5.6.

The generate-and-test approach taken by the system to determine whether a particular feature is critical or not is inefficient compared to some alternative approaches based on analytically examining the LOOM definition and determining the features from there. Unfortunately, a purely analytical approach is not possible in our case, because certain constructs such as the kleene-closure in BNF cannot be represented in the LOOM semantics. Since these constructs are essential,

---

[4]In Book Two of his *De Copia*, Erasmus discusses the need for selection of features that will be very significant in the examples presented. In the "method of presenting proofs and arguments", he goes on to say: "A most effective means ... is to be found in illustrative examples .... The content of the examples can be something like, unlike, or in contrast to, what we are illustrating."

[5]It is possible that these modifications will not be applicable in many domains; the alternative (to not using such domain specific modification information) is to use a representation as in CEG (Suthers and Rissland, 1988), where every concept contained annotations on how various features could be modified.

they are represented as predicates in LISP that are used by LOOM during classification and matching. These predicates thus cannot be examined analytically to determine the critical and variable features, and it is therefore necessary to use the generate-and-test approach to classify the features as such. The representation of a list in LISP, which is defined using a kleene-closure, will be seen in chapter 6.

There are a total of seven ways along two dimensions with which the system attempts to modify each feature of a concept definition in this domain to try and find a critical feature. Two of these seven variations are with respect to the *number* dimension; the remaining five are with respect to the *type* dimension. We shall illustrate the working of the algorithm by taking the example of the concept list in the LISP domain. In the case of the introductory text type, the system retrieves the syntactic, surface features for presentation. These are the left parenthesis, the data elements, and the right parenthesis. Given these three features, the system must now determine which of these features are critical and which are variable. The system attempts to generate and test different instances created from modifying the definition of a list. As stated here, the system attempts to modify features along two dimensions:

Number Dimension: First, the system attempts to see if deleting the feature under consideration from the definition causes the system to classify this modified instance wrongly. If it does, the feature is marked as being critical. Secondly, the system checks to see whether adding an extra element identical to the feature causes the system to find the modified instance as belonging to another class. In both these cases, the fact that the feature is critical with regard to the number is noted by the system. Thus, if the BNF definition is of the form:

$$\mathbf{A} - grammar\text{-}seq - \mathbf{B} - grammar\text{-}seq - \mathbf{C}$$

the system successively considers modified definitions of the form:

$$\mathbf{A} - grammar\text{-}seq - \mathbf{A} - grammar\text{-}seq - \mathbf{B} - grammar\text{-}seq - \mathbf{C}$$
$$\mathbf{A} - grammar\text{-}seq - \mathbf{B} - grammar\text{-}seq - \mathbf{B} - grammar\text{-}seq - \mathbf{C}$$
$$\mathbf{A} - grammar\text{-}seq - \mathbf{B} - grammar\text{-}seq - \mathbf{C} - grammar\text{-}seq - \mathbf{C}$$
$$\mathbf{A} - grammar\text{-}seq - \mathbf{C} - grammar\text{-}seq - \mathbf{B} - grammar\text{-}seq - \mathbf{C}$$

$$\vdots$$

For each feature in the set of input features, determine if the feature is a critical feature by creating an instance of a modified definition and checking whether the (modified) instance classifies under the original definition. The modified definitions are created by varying each feature in the definition as follows:

1. *Varying the Number:*

   (a) modify the definition by omitting the feature from the definition

   (b) modify the definition by adding another symbol of the same type as the current symbol in the definition

   if in either of these two cases, the modified instance fails to classify under the original definition, mark the feature as being critical along the number dimension.

2. *Varying the Type:*

   if the feature is a terminal symbol:

   (a) modify the definition by substituting the feature with another terminal symbol of the same type

   (b) modify the definition by substituting the feature with a terminal symbol of another type

   else if the feature is a non-terminal symbol:

   (a) modify the definition by substituting the feature with the superconcept of the feature

   (b) modify the definition by substituting the feature with the subconcept of the feature

   (c) modify the definition by substituting the feature with the sibling concept of the feature

   if, in any of these cases, the modified instance fails to classify under the original definition, mark the type of the feature as a critical feature.

Figure 5.6: Determining the critical features of a concept in BNF.

and checks if the modified concept description still classifies as a sub-concept of the original concept.

For the case of a list, instances of a list are created from modi-fied definitions and tested to see whether they classify under the orig-inal definition of a list. Modifications along the number dimension, such as reducing the number of parentheses by one, or adding an ex-tra parenthesis, cause the instances to not classify under the original definition. Thus, both the left and the right parentheses are marked as critical.[6] On the other hand, modifications to the number of data elements in the list, by either deleting one, or adding one, do not result in the instance failing to classify as a list. At this point therefore, the data elements are not classified as critical features.

Type Dimension: There are a number of different ways in which the system attempts to modify a feature by varying the type dimension:

Terminals: If the feature being considered happens to be a terminal symbol (the POPART-to-LOOM transformer marks the grammar sym-bols appropriately as being terminal and non-terminal symbols based on their BNF representation), the system modifies the definition of the concept in two ways: (1) by replacing the symbol with another terminal symbol of the same type. For instance, if the terminal symbol hap-pened to be a number, 2 for example, the system would try to replace 2 with another number, for instance, 7, and (2) by replacing the terminal symbol with another terminal symbol of another type. For instance, in the previous case, the system could attempt to replace the number 2 with a character, such as 'a'. In the case of the list, the system can attempt to replace the left-parenthesis with another terminal symbol, such as the right-parenthesis, and in the second case, by a keyword, such as 'defun'. If in either of these cases, an instance of the modified definition did not classify as an instance of the original definition, the system would mark the fact that the type of the feature was a critical feature.

Non-Terminals: If the feature being considered is a non-terminal symbol, the system attempts to modify the definition by changing the symbol in three different ways: (1) by replacing it with a superconcept,

---

[6]Currently, the system does not attempt to vary more than one feature at a time while trying to determine the nature of the features. Thus, the system does not attempt to add/delete both the parentheses and see whether the resulting construct would still classify as a list or something else.

(2) by replacing it with a sub-concept, and (3) by replacing it with a sibling concept. In the case of the list, case 1 is not applicable, because data-element is the most general type in the representation of a list, because it is the disjunction of the symbol, number, and list types; case 2 could result in the system replacing data-element with another type such as number, and case 3 is again not applicable in the case of data-element. Because a list of numbers is still a valid list, the type aspect of data-elements is not marked as being a critical feature for a list.

The algorithm is also given in figure 5.6.[7] The algorithm allows the system to determine the critical features of a concept. Once these features have been determined, the system caches these values so that it does not have to repeat this reasoning the next time it has to determine critical features for the same object and is given the same set of input features.

As in the case of get-example, the function to find the critical features of an object has been designed for use as a function in the CONSTRAINTS of a text plan operator. The function is given a list of features and an object, and returns those features from the set that are critical. A typical call is shown below:

function: select-critical-features
```
(select-critical-features ?features ?object)
```

typical call:
```
(select-critical-features
   '(left-parenthesis
     (kleene-closure data-elements)
     right-parenthesis)
   'list)
```

In this case, the function call returns:

```
(left-parenthesis right-parenthesis)
```

---

[7]Note that this algorithm is a superset of the algorithm used by LEX (Mitchell, Utgoff, and Banerji, 1983) to generate new problems: LEX only attempted substitution of a term with a sibling term.

The function *selects* critical features from a list of features passed to it, rather than *finding* the critical features, because different cases may require the presentation of different sets of features. For instance, the generation of descriptions for introductory and advanced texts requires the presentation of quite different amounts and types of information in many domains. Thus, in our system, the constraints in the plan operator first select the appropriate features for the given text type from the LOOM representation, and then, determine the critical features from this set of features to be presented.

5.3.3   Determining Variable Features

As in the case of critical features, the system must know which features are variable in nature. A knowledge of the variable features then allows the system to illustrate the variability by presenting multiple positive examples that vary in the variable features. Because variable features are not critical features, if the critical features for a concept are known, the system can attempt to prune the set of features to be considered by removing the critical features.[8] The remaining features are then processed exactly in the same manner in which the critical features are determined; the only difference is that the systems tests for successful classification (rather than a failure to classify) after each modification. Each feature is varied along both the type, and the number dimensions, as in the previous case, regarding the critical features:

- **Number Dimension:**

  - vary the definition by omitting the current feature from the definition.

  - vary the definition by adding another feature of the same type as the current feature.

- **Type Dimension:**

  - if feature is a terminal: attempt replacements with (a) other terminals of the same type, and (b) terminals of another type.

---

[8]The reasoning mechanism which determines the critical features also uses this null intersection criteria to prune the set of features it has to consider in finding critical features.

– if feature is a non-terminal: attempt replacements with subtype, supertype and sibling types.

If instances created from the modified definitions still classify under the original definition of the concept, the feature is marked appropriately as a variable feature. As we mentioned previously, LOOM allows us to determine the class of the description very simply with its classification mechanism. As in the case of critical features, the variable features of the object are cached upon computation so that future calls to the function can be answered using simple retrieves.

Features of a concept can be critical and variable at the same time– along different dimensions. Consider the case of the operator PLUS in LISP for instance. Although the number of arguments that follow the operator are not critical, the type of the arguments is — they should be numbers. Similarly, in the case of the operator CONS in LISP, the number of arguments is critical, although their type is not. It is therefore important to identify not just whether a feature is critical or variable,[9] but also in what respect.

5.3.4 Finding Interesting Negative Examples

An important aspect in generating tutorial descriptions is the presentation of negative examples. Negative examples need to be presented to highlight the critical aspects of the concept being described. However, since there can be different negative examples that can be used in any given situation, it is beneficial to use examples that are "interesting" in some sense, rather than any random example. Consider for instance, the case of a list in figure 5.7. In this case, let us consider the two parentheses (left and right), as being one atomic unit in the grammar; i.e., the parentheses are either removed, or added, only as pairs. In the two pairs of positive–negative examples presented there, both the pairs emphasize the critical nature of the parentheses. However, the

---

[9]All features are either critical or variable, depending on their role in the concept definition. However, some critical features, such as parentheses in LISP are so ubiquitous that they can be a distraction when discussing complex constructs. To handle this aspect, we shall introduce the concept of *fixed features*, which are critical features and therefore appear in all examples, but are not explicitly used by the system to generate negative examples, or commented upon. We shall see an example of these fixed features in chapter 7.

```
(GREEN GRASS BLUE SKIES)      ;   list of symbols
 GREEN GRASS BLUE SKIES       ;   not a list

(AARDVARK)                    ;   a list of one symbol
 AARDVARK                     ;   an atom, not a list
```

Figure 5.7: Negative examples can serve multiple roles: (a) *not* being an example of the concept being illustrated, and also (b) illustrating another *concept* that might be confused by the user.

---

second pair of examples is more pedagogical, because it conveys not only the fact that the negative example is not a list, but *also* that it is an atom. It is therefore important to find such interesting negative examples, if they are available. Note also that this allows the system to opportunistically include more material if so desired (with a CONTRAST relation).

In our system, finding interesting negative examples is made quite easy using the classification mechanism in LOOM. Each time the system finds a critical feature, it tests to see if the modification causing the example to become negative also causes the example to classify under *another* description in the knowledge base. If it does, the system marks this critical feature, as well as the classification of the negative example, and uses this in preference to some other example.

This method of finding interesting negative examples is very dependent on the availablity of a *classification mechanism*.[10] Whereas the previously mentioned use of LOOM (in determining critical and variable features) could easily be implemented even without the use of a classifier, finding interesting negative examples would be much harder to implement without this capability.

The complexity of the feature ftr is defined as:

1. if $terminal(ftr)$ then $complexity(ftr) = 1$

2. if $non\text{-}terminal(ftr)$ and the right-hand side (RHS) of the grammar production is a disjunction, then $complexity(ftr)$ is equal to the sum of the complexities of the types in the disjunction on the RHS.

3. if $non\text{-}terminal(ftr)$ and the RHS of the production is not a disjunction, then $complexity(ftr)$ is equal to the product of the complexities of each of the elements in the RHS.

4. if $kleene\text{-}closure(ftr)$, and the ftr is defined as a disjunction of n types, then $complexity(ftr)$ is equal to

$$2^{n-1} * complexity(type_1) + \cdots + 2^{n-1} * complexity(type_n)$$

5. if $recursive(ftr)$ then $complexity(ftr) = \infty$

Figure 5.8: Determining syntactic complexity of a term in the BNF domain.

5.3.5 Example Complexity and Sequencing

An important issue in the presentation of examples is the issue of sequencing their presentation appropriately. As discussed in section 3.6, the order of presentation is, in general, dependent on the relative complexity of the features of the concept to be presented. There are two levels at which the sequencing needs to be planned:

- at the *feature* level: where the system must decide the features that need to be presented first. This will determine the presentation order of example sets illustrating each feature.

- at the individual *example* level, where the system must determine how examples *within* each example set (illustrating a feature) need to be sequenced.

The complexity of a feature, or a concept in a domain, cannot be determined completely independently of the domain: in our case (using BNF grammars for programming languages), the syntactic complexity of a particular construct is computed as follows:

- if the feature is a terminal symbol, the complexity measure of that feature is considered to be 1. Thus, the complexity measures of terminal symbols such as left-parenthesis, characters, such as a, b, and numbers such as 5 and 7, are all 1. This is because a terminal symbol can be considered a constant and needs only one example to illustrate.

- if the feature is a non-terminal symbol where the non-terminal symbol is a disjunction of different types, then the complexity measure of the feature is the sum of the complexity measures of the components in the disjunction. For instance, if data-element is a non-terminal defined as follows:

```
data-element := symbol | number | string |
                character | list;
```

---

[10]Classification, or structural subsumption, is theoretically undecidable (Doyle and Patil, 1991). However, in practice, exponential algorithms exist that determine, for certain restricted languages, whether one description logically entails another.

then the complexity measure of data-element is defined to be the sum of the complexity-measures of symbol, number, string, character, and list.

This is because the number of examples that would be required to communicate the different features of the non-terminal on the lefthand side of the production would be equal to the sum of the examples required for each of the righthand side elements. In the simplest case, if the right hand side consisted only of a number of terminal symbols, the complexity of the non-terminal on the lefthand side would be the number of terminals in the disjunction.

- if the feature is a non-terminal symbol which is not defined as a disjunction, then the complexity of the symbol is the product of the complexity of each of the elements in righthand side (RHS) of the production. In this case, the complexity reflects the fact that the total number of examples needed to illustrate this non-terminal would be the total number of legal permutations possible for the production. For instance, consider the definition of a list:

```
list := left-parenthesis
        { data-elements + }
        right-parenthesis;
```

In this case, the complexity measure of the symbol list is the product of the complexity measures of a left-parenthesis, the term '{data-element +}' and the right-parenthesis.

- the complexity of a kleene-closure of a symbol (such as {data-elements +}), is computed by calculating the sum of the products of the complexity of each of the symbol's derived types, and the number of examples that each of these derived types can occur in. Since a kleene-closure of a symbol represents the power set of all of the symbol's derived types, the total number of examples that a particular type can appear in is 2^{n-1} where n is the total number of derived types. For example, the complexity of the kleene-closure of data-element (the expression '{data-element +}'), could be computed as follows. If the concept data-elements is defined as a disjunction:

```
data-elements := symbol | number | list;
```

the derived types are: (a) symbols, (b) numbers and (c) lists, and n is equal to 3.

$$\text{complexity}(\{\texttt{data-elements +}\}) = \begin{cases} 2^2 * \text{complexity}(\texttt{symbol}) \\ + \\ 2^2 * \text{complexity}(\texttt{number}) \\ + \\ 2^2 * \text{complexity}(\texttt{list}) \end{cases}$$

The rationale for this complexity measure lies in the fact that a kleene-closure can vary in two dimensions: (a) in the number of elements per set, and (b) the type of elements in each set. Thus, the total number of examples necessary for illustrating a term defined as a kleene-closure is the total number of examples in the power set, plus the additional examples generated due to the variable nature of each of the derived terms that are part of the examples. If the complexity measure of each of the derived types is 1 (for instance, if all of the derived types were terminal symbols), then the complexity of the term under consideration is equal to 2^n, where n is the number of derived types (this represents the power set of the derived types).

- if the feature is a recursive non-terminal (i.e., the non-terminal on the lefthand side of the production also appears on the right-hand side of the production), then the complexity of the feature is considered to be *infinity*. This is because the feature can potentially need an infinite number of examples to illustrate all the possible cases.

The algorithm is summarized in figure 5.8. The algorithm is invoked by the top-level function ORDER-BY-COMPLEXITY, which is the function used in the CONSTRAINTS of the plan operators. This function also takes into account certain annotations that indicate whether the feature is a variable one. In the case of variable features, there are two ways that they can vary: the *number* and the *type*. Given the goal of generating examples for two variable aspects of a feature, the system compares the relative complexity of the two features. For instance, in illustrating the variable nature of data-element of a list, the function would compare the complexity of the number aspect and the type aspect for data elements. The *number* aspect is computed as 2 (one example at each end of the range is desired to illustrate the variable nature: one with a small number of elements, and another with a large number of elements). The complexity of the *type* aspect is computed by finding the number of subtypes of the given feature. This is because the system needs to present at least one example of each sub-type. The ordering of the presentation is then done on the basis of their relative complexities. In the case of the `data-elements` given above, since the type complexity is greater than 2, examples illustrating the variable nature of the *number* aspect are presented before the examples illustrating the *type* aspect.

Apart from the complexity measure mentioned above, there is one more constraint that can sometimes influence the order in which examples are presented: if there is a *significant* negative example that the system needs to present to the user, and the text type is introductory, the system will need to generate additional text discussing the negative example (and its differences with the *close* positive example). In this case, the system orders the examples such that the positive–interesting-negative example pair is the last pair presented in the sequence. This allows the system to present all the positive examples together, before presenting a discussion of the interesting negative example. (An instance of this case will be seen in section 7.3.)

5.3.6   Generating Prompts

There is another aspect of the presentation that must be dealt with at the same time as the example generation. This is the issue of presenting prompts. As mentioned earlier (in section 3.8), prompts are meant to convey additional information that can help focus the user's attention; while they can be pictorial, formatting directives (such as bold-face fonts, changes in color, and so on.), or even animated characters, we only consider here the use of short phrases in text to achieve our purpose. Prompts are essential if the examples illustrate multiple features at the same time. Prompts become necessary:

- if the example retrieved by the system in response to a communicative goal happens to possess *more* (or *less* in the case of a negative example) features than the communicative goal specified; this can be determined by analysing the number of variable features that a positive example possesses (positive examples will possess all critical features) and comparing them with what was asked for; in the case of a negative example, since a negative example may be deficient in more than one critical feature, the numbers of both critical and variable features need to be observed. If the number of features in the goal and the examples generated do not match, it is desirable that prompts be generated to highlight those features in the examples that the goal was supposed to illustrate. In our system, this will result in generation of a prompt.

- if the examples are presented physically far away from the point where the concept being illustrated is mentioned in the textual description. This is one of the reasons why prompts are seen so often in reference manual style texts, because the text type prevents the generation of examples until the description is complete: this often results, in the case of long descriptions, in examples being placed away from the concept's mention.

- if the example is a result of combining more than one communicative goal: this may be either by design, as in the case of reference manual style texts, where goals to illustrate individual features are combined at the end to present one or two complex multi-featured examples, or serendipitously (as in the case of the planner finding two adjacent speech acts presenting examples that can fulfill each other's goal: an example of this occurs in a description of a list presented in the following chapter, where the following two goals are generated adjacent to each other in the discourse structure:

```
(PRESENT-EXAMPLE LIST (DATA-ELEMENT (NUMBER MULTIPLE)))
(PRESENT-EXAMPLE LIST (DATA-ELEMENT (TYPE ATOMS)))
```

The first goal occurs as a result of another goal that illustrates how examples can contain different numbers of elements; as it happens, the planner generates an example of multiple elements that are *all atoms* to satisfy the goal. This example meets the requirements of the next goal, which specifies the need to generate an example of a list of atoms. In such cases, if the system folds these two goals into one, it needs to generate a prompt to highlight the fact that two features are being illustrated).

- It is also essential to explicitly mark an example as being either anomalous or exceptionally difficult (for instance recursive constructions of a concept, such as a list of lists): such marking can be done either through the use of prompts, or through the generation of appropriate background text before the example is actually presented. In introductory texts, the system usually generates background text; in the case of advanced texts, prompts are preferred over text, to explain the examples.

5.4 Discussion

Our framework is centered around a text planner that generates text and posts explicit goals to generate examples that are included in the description. Plans also indicate how and when to generate the prompt information. By appropriately modifying the constraints on each plan operator, we can investigate the effects of different resources in the framework. Our example generator uses the classifier mechanism in LOOM to determine critical and variable features, as well as interesting negative examples. We have devised a complexity heuristic for the BNF domain that works well in our application. We use this complexity information to devise the ordering of the examples in the presentation at the global level.

The system contains about 60 plan operators that generate descriptions with integrated text and examples. The operators can model various interaction effects between text and examples such as the introduction of "interesting" negative examples in both LISP and the INTEND domains. The operators have been tested by planning the description of numerous syntactic constructs in programming languages such as LISP, INTEND and JAVA; some of these are shown in appendix D. The discourse structures generated were checked for correctness, and also whether the system had found the all the critical and variable features.

The system is currently unable to generate meaningful descriptions for constructs where the syntax does not contain enough information. For instance, the let-form is defined in INTEND as:

```
let-form := '( 'LET '( { let-binding + } ')
                    expression + ') ;
```

In this case, there is no further information that the variables defined in the let-binding should appear in the expression. Consequently, the system generates a description that does not reflect user expectations. Similarly, the `loop` statement is defined as:

```
loop-form := ' ( 'LOOP { loop-with }
                      { loop-initially }
                      { iteration-driving-clause + }
                      { loop-condition-clause + }
                      { loop-action-form }
                      { loop-finally } ') ;
```

However, the relationship between each of the components of a `loop` are not specified, and the system is unable to generate useful explanations about it. This illustrates one of the major shortcomings of this implementation: it does not, as yet, represent any semantic information about the various constructs in the domain. This results in an inability to generate descriptions at present that are either "use" oriented, and so depend upon the underlying semantics, as seen in intermediate texts, or in generating even purely syntactic descriptions where different parts of the syntactic specification interact with each other in ways that are not captured by the BNF. These and other limitations of our current implementation are discussed further in section 10.2. If this system is to be scaled up, the semantics of the constructs must be represented as well.

In the following chapters, we illustrate the working of the system by generating descriptions about LISP, as well as INTEND, about some constructs for which the system can generate useful descriptions.

Chapter 6

Generating Descriptions

Example is always more efficacious than precept.

– Samuel Johnson

The previous chapter described the text planner and example generator components of the system. In this section, we illustrate the working
of the system by tracing through the generation of three descriptions
for the same concept, a list in LISP. The descriptions are in the text-
only mode, examples-only mode, and with both text and examples. This
will clarify many of the issues that were presented earlier.

We have already mentioned that the BNF descriptions are converted
to an equivalent LOOM representation for use in the system. In most
cases, this transformation is straightforward, as in the illustrations
given in section 5.2. Occasionally, however, certain constructs are more
difficult to translate. The *kleene-closure* is one example of a construct
that maps differently into LOOM. Consider the POPART and LOOM descriptions of a list as given in figures 6.1 and 6.2.

The LOOM description of the list requires that a LISP predicate,
the function 'loom-list-p' (given in figure 6.3), be used to determine
whether a given instance classifies under the description or not. This
is because of the fact that effects such as kleene-closures are difficult to
specify in languages such as LOOM (Patil, 1993). However, this results
in a LOOM definition that cannot be easily used by the text planner

```
list := ‘( {data-element *} ’) ;

data-element := symbol | number | character | list ;
```

Figure 6.1: Description of a list in POPART.

```
(defconcept data-element
   :is (:or symbol number character list))

(defconcept list
   :is (:and grammar-symbol
             (:predicate (?x)
                   (loom-list-p ?x)))))
```

Figure 6.2: Description of a list in LOOM.

```
(defun LOOM-LIST-P (x)
   (declare (special parens no-error))
   (setf no-error t)
   (cond ((loom-type-p x 'left-parenthesis)
          (setf parens 1)
          (loom-list-1-p (get-range x 'grammar-sequence))
          (and no-error (zerop parens)))
         (t nil)))

(defun LOOM-LIST-1-P (x)
   (cond ((null x) nil)
         ((loom-type-p x 'left-parenthesis)
          (setf parens (+ parens 1)))
         ((loom-type-p x 'data-elements))
         ((loom-type-p x 'right-parenthesis)
          (setf parens (- parens 1)))
         (t (setf no-error nil)))
   (if (and x (get-range x 'grammar-sequence))
       (loom-list-1-p (get-range x 'grammar-sequence)))))
```

Figure 6.3: Predicate used by LOOM to check for list.

```
(defconcept list
  :is (:and grammar-symbol
            (:predicate (?x) (loom-list-p ?x)))
  :annotations
    ((syntax
        (left-parenthesis (kleene-closure data-elements)
                          right-parenthesis)))))
```

Figure 6.4: LOOM description of a list.

(which expects LOOM relations and concepts and is unable to explain LISP code). It is thus necessary to add the structural and syntactic information about lists that the text planner expects and needs to generate from. In our domain, the list concept is represented as shown in figure 6.4. With this definition of a list, we present three scenarios where the system generates presentations that consist of text only, examples only, and both text and examples. The target text type is introductory, so examples are generated wherever possible, usually interspersed within the description. This will illustrate the integration between text and examples.

6.1   A Purely Textual Description of LIST

To generate a description for the concept list, the system starts with an initial top level goal of (BEL HEARER (CONCEPT LIST)).[1] Two of the plan operators in the plan library that match this goal (i.e., their EFFECT slot is specified as (BEL HEARER (CONCEPT ?OBJECT)) and the variable ?object can be bound to list) are shown in figure 6.5.

Both the plan operators in figure 6.5 can be used by the system to describe objects: the first plan operator is used to generate descriptions that have some textual explanation, with or without examples; the sec-

---

[1] In our initial implementation, the goal form contained the term NOUN, which in the DIM model (Engelmann and Carnine, 1982), represents a multifeatured basic form.

ond plan operator is used to generate descriptions that have only examples. The first plan operator checks whether the object is a term in
the grammar, and then finds the appropriate text type[2] to use for the
object. This is done using a simple user model, which contains the objects the user is familiar with. If the object being described appears in
the user model, the system selects the advanced text type, otherwise,
the system generates an introductory text. In our current scenario, the
user model contains only atom, and number. Thus, the system selects
an introductory text type for generation. The constraints then cause
the selection of appropriate features to be presented to the user. In this
case, the text type cause surface, syntactic features to be selected for
presentation. The plan operator also specifies that the object is to be
described by first listing the features, and then elaborating upon each
one of them.

The second plan operator is discarded by the system because the
use-examples-only constraint is not satisfied in the context. This
plan operator is therefore inapplicable in the given situation.

The constraints in the plan operator selected bind the variable ?ftrs
to the syntactic features of a list. This is because the text type is
specified as introductory (the differences between introductory and advanced text types are discussed in greater detail in chapter 8). The
system posts appropriate goals for both the NUCLEUS and the SATEL-
LITE:

NUCLEUS:
```
(BEL HEARER
     (FTRS-LIST (left-parenthesis
                 (kleene-closure data-elements)
                 right-parenthesis)
      list))
```

SATELLITE:
```
(ELABORATE left-parenthesis list)
(ELABORATE (kleene-closure data-elements) list)
(ELABORATE right-parenthesis list)
```

---

[2]In this implementation, we have not considered the generation of intermediate texts.

```
(define-text-plan-operator
   :EFFECT (bel hearer (concept ?object))
   :CONSTRAINTS
     (and
       (isa? ?object grammar-object)
       (get-text-type-for-object ?text-type ?object)
       (get-appropriate-ftrs ?ftrs ?object ?text-type)
       (not *use-examples-only*))
   :NUCLEUS (bel hearer (ftrs-list ?ftrs ?object))
   :SATELLITES (((foreach ?ftrs
                   (elaboration ?ftrs ?object)) *optional*)))
```

```
(define-text-plan-operator
   :EFFECT (bel hearer (concept ?object))
   :CONSTRAINTS
     (and
       (isa? ?object grammar-object)
       (get-text-type-for-object ?text-type ?object)
       (get-appropriate-ftrs ?ftrs ?object ?user)
       (select-critical-ftrs ?crit-ftrs ?ftrs ?object)
       (enumerate-ftrs ?ex-crit-ftrs ?crit-ftrs ?object)
       (order-by-complexity ?eg-crit-ftrs ?ex-crit-ftrs)
       (select-variable-ftrs ?var-ftrs ?ftrs ?object)
       (enumerate-ftrs ?ex-var-ftrs ?var-ftrs ?object)
       (order-by-complexity ?eg-var-ftrs ?ex-var-ftrs)
       *use-examples-only*)
   :NUCLEUS
     ((foreach ?eg-var-ftrs
         (bel hearer (example-seq ?eg-var-ftrs ?object)))
      (foreach ?eg-crit-ftrs
         (bel hearer (example-pair ?eg-crit-ftrs ?object))))
   :SATELLITES
     (((background
         (present-eg-background ?object)) *optional*)))
```

Figure 6.5: Top level plan operators to describe objects.

The relation ELABORATE appears in each of the subgoals posted as a SATELLITE; as we mentioned earlier, the presence of appropriate coherence relations between the text spans allows for the insertion of appropriate cue phrases to ensure that the final text is coherent.

The planner looks for applicable plan operators for the first subgoal, the one posted by the NUCLEUS.[3] The system finds two plan operators that have applicable :EFFECT specifications: one of the plan operators is meant for listing a single feature; the other one is meant for goals listing multiple features. Because there are three features to be listed in this case, the second plan operator is selected for this subgoal. This goal in turn, posts further subgoals that finally result in the posting of three primitive goals which mention each of the three features. Each of these subgoals is an INFORM ... goal, or a speech-act, that can be realized in English without further planning. These three subgoals are linked to each other through the SEQUENCE relation, which here indicates the ordering of the syntactic elements. The SEQUENCE relation causes the realization component to insert the cue phrase "followed by" between the phrases generated by the primitive goals. The text plan generated so far appears in figure 6.6.[4] At this point, the system can generate the following sentence, that mentions all the features of a list:

> A list consists of a left parenthesis, followed by zero or more data elements, followed by a right parenthesis.

The system still needs to expand the goals which were posted as the SATELLITE goals of the original top-level goal:

SATELLITE:
```
(ELABORATE left-parenthesis list)
(ELABORATE (kleene-closure data-elements) list)
(ELABORATE right-parenthesis list)
```

The system attempts each of these (optional) goals in turn. It fails to find further information in the domain model for the left-parenthesis

---

[3]In most cases, the NUCLEUS subgoals are generated first, before the satellite subgoals; however, certain RST relations, such as BACKGROUND and PURPOSE specify that the SATELLITE text should be generated before the nucleus subgoal is expanded.

[4]The text plans shown here are simplified to show the communicative goals without the formal notation.

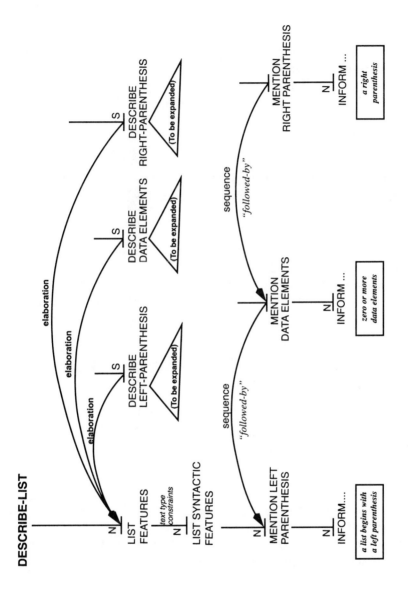

Figure 6.6: Plan skeleton for listing the main features of a list.

and is therefore unable to expand on this feature. Since the satellite was marked *optional*, the system does not try to backtrack up to the parent node (to describe a list). The second SATELLITE goal is to elaborate upon the kleene closure of data-elements in a list. The system determines, based on the domain model, that data-elements of a list can be of different types: symbols, numbers, or lists. It therefore expands this goal by generating a speech act which is an INFORM goal about the kleen closure of symbols, numbers or lists. Since this is a primitive goal, it is not expanded further. The third satellite goal, to elaborate upon the right parenthesis also fails due to a lack of further domain knowledge. Thus, the top level satellite goals result in a speech act that represents the fact that data elements of a list can be kleene closures of a set that contains symbols, numbers or other lists.

The resulting discourse structure is then processed by the grammar interface and the sentence generator. The resulting output, with appropriate connectives generated because of the coherence relations, is shown in figure 6.7. The figure contains a screen snapshot of the system showing the complete text plan (with goals and plan operator names truncated after 20 characters), as well as the resulting description.

6.2   Describing a LIST Using Only Examples

The previous section showed the system generating a purely textual description of a list in LISP. An alternative description of a list can be one where the system generates only examples, without any accompanying explanation.

Because the system must communicate all the features through examples only, the system must first categorize *each* feature as being either a *critical* feature, or a *variable* feature. This is necessary because critical and variable features are communicated using different strategies: critical features through the pairing of minimally different[5] positive and negative examples, and variable features through the presentation of groups of widely differing positive examples.[6] The system must then also order these examples for presentation to the user.

---

[5]The difference is in the presence and absence of the critical feature.

[6]The examples are identical except in the varying feature, which is widely varied.

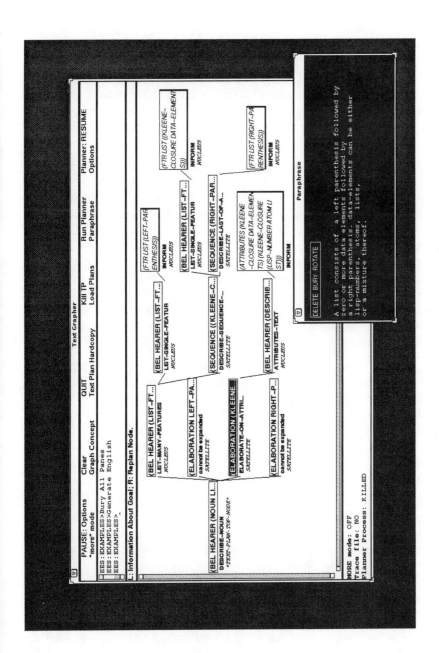

Figure 6.7: A purely textual description of a list.

In the case of a `list`, there are only three features that can be expressed through examples: the left parenthesis, the data elements and the right parenthesis. The system determines (using the algorithm given in sections 5.3.2 and 5.3.3) that the left parenthesis and the right parenthesis are critical features, because the instances that the system created without these features did not classify as instances of a `list`, whereas modifying the data-elements in different instances did not cause the instances to not classify as a `list`.

The system must also determine the order in which examples illustrating different features are to be presented: it does this ordering within each group (critical features and variable features) using the algorithm presented in section 5.3.5. Since both the left and the right parentheses are equally complex according to the algorithm, the system presents them without any particular ordering. Since the concept `data-elements` is a non-terminal, the system first determines its sub-types (symbols, numbers and lists), finds the kleene closure (the power set of these 3 sub-types) and orders them in increasing complexity (again, using the algorithm in section 5.3.5). The system must also ensure during the presentation of the variable features that it generates examples with varying number of elements in them.

Finally, the system determines whether the number of examples required to communicate the critical features is more than the number of examples required to communicate the variable features. Since the variable features require more examples, the system presents examples illustrating the critical features before the variable features. This can be seen in the constraints of the plan operator in figure 6.8.[7] The plan operator posts a goal to present a pair of examples for each critical feature, and a set of examples for the variable features.

It may seem that because critical features are important in the examples that the critical features should be presented first, before the variable features. Although most of the texts in the corpus do display this phenomenon (critical features being presented first), we believe

---

[7]The original EES text planner used to post goals in reverse order, i.e., if there were two goals in the NUCLEUS, the system would first post the goal that appeared second in the NUCLEUS. Thus, the actual plan operator in the system had the goals in the NUCLEUS reversed; however, for clarity, we have presented the goals here in the more conventional order. Of course, it is possible to deal with the ordering issue in a more principled fashion by having a module that explicitly reasons about goal and clause ordering either during the text planning phase, or during the microplanning phase.

```
(define-text-plan-operator
   :EFFECT (BEL HEARER (NOUN ?OBJECT))
   :CONSTRAINTS
      (and
         (isa? ?object concept)
         (get-user-type-for-object ?user-type ?object)
         (get-appropriate-ftrs  ?ftrs ?object ?user-type)
         (select-critical-ftrs ?crit-ftrs ?ftrs ?object)
         (enumerate-ftrs ?ex-crit-ftrs ?crit-ftrs ?object)
         (order-by-complexity ?eg-crit-ftrs ?ex-crit-ftrs)
         (select-variable-ftrs ?var-ftrs ?ftrs ?object)
         (enumerate-ftrs ?ex-var-ftrs ?var-ftrs ?object)
         (order-by-complexity ?eg-var-ftrs ?ex-var-ftrs)
         (complexity-greater ?eg-crit-ftrs ?eg-var-ftrs)
         *USE-EXAMPLES-ONLY*)
   :NUCLEUS
      ((FOREACH ?EG-CRIT-FTRS
           (bel hearer (example-pair ?eg-crit-ftrs ?object)))
       (FOREACH ?EG-VAR-FTRS
           (bel hearer (example-seq  ?eg-var-ftrs  ?object))))
   :SATELLITES
      (((BACKGROUND
           (eg-background ?object))  *optional*)))
```

Figure 6.8: Plan Operator to generate example-only descriptions.

that the ordering of the features is actually caused by the fact that the number of examples necessary to illustrate the critical features in most cases are less than the number of examples necessary to illustrate the variable features, and thus according to our complexity heuristic, are presented first. It is also sometimes not possible to present critical features first, because the presence of significant negative examples could cause the generation of further explanation, which should be sequenced last. Because the positive and negative examples should be presented adjacent to each other in the presentation sequence, that critical feature then gets presented last.

Since the examples are presented on their own, with no accompanying description, the system must also present prompts with the examples. The prompts should, at the very least identify the examples as being either positive or negative. In this case, if more than one feature is being illustrated, the system generates prompts which contain information about the types of data elements in the list. The resulting text plan and description are shown in figures 6.9 and 6.10. The first four examples in the output are due to the critical features. The remaining examples are due to the variable features: a list of atoms, a list of numbers, a list of atoms and numbers, a list of a list, and so forth. The system did not present negative examples of atoms (by stripping the parentheses) because as we stated earlier, the system only attempts to determine critical and variable features by modifying the original definition *one feature at a time*.

6.3 Generating an Integrated Description of LIST

Let us see how the system generates an integrated description containing both text and examples. The system initially begins (as in the previous two cases) with the top-level goal being given as (BEL HEARER (CONCEPT LIST)). The text planner searches for applicable plan operators in its plan library, and it picks one based on the EFFECT statement and the applicable constraints. The plan operator selected is the same plan operator initially selected when the system generated a purely textual description of a list. The text type causes the syntactic features of the list to be selected for presentation, as in section 6.1. The main features of list are retrieved, and two subgoals are posted: one to list all the features (the left parenthesis, the data elements and the right parenthesis), and another to elaborate on them.

At this point, the discourse tree has only three nodes: the initial node of (BEL HEARER (CONCEPT LIST)),[8] and its two children nodes: (1) LIST-FEATURES, and (2) DESCRIBE-FEATURES, which are linked by a coherence relation, ELABORATE.

The text-planner now has one NUCLEUS and three SATELLITE goals to expand:

---

[8]For the sake of clarity, we shall refer to such goals as (DESCRIBE-...).

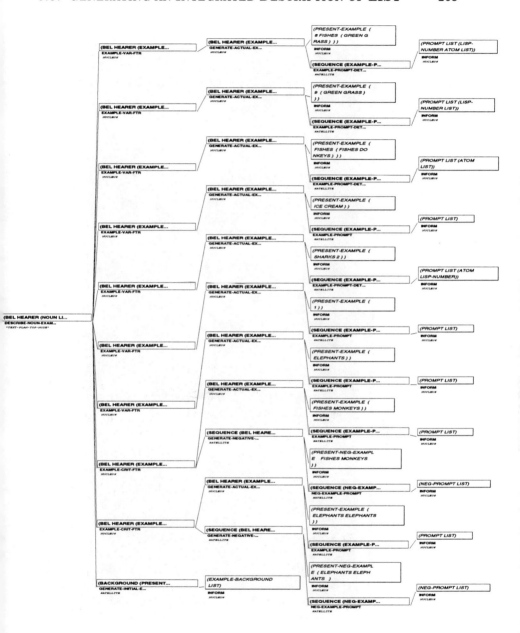

Figure 6.9: Text plan generated for the examples-only description of list.

Examples

DELETE BURY ROTATE

```
Examples of LIST are:

( ELEPHANTS ELEPHANTS )          ; An example of LIST
( ELEPHANTS ELEPHANTS            ; not a LIST
( FISHES MONKEYS )               ; Another example of LIST
( FISHES MONKEYS )               ; not a LIST
( ELEPHANTS )                    ; Another example of LIST
( 1 )                            ; Another example of LIST
( SHARKS 2 )                     ; A LIST of a atom, and a lisp-number.
( ICE CREAM )                    ; Another example of LIST
( FISHES  ( FISHES DONKEYS ) )   ; A LIST of a atom, and a list.
( 9  ( GREEN GRASS ) )           ; A LIST of a lisp-number, and a list.
( 8 FISHES ( GREEN GRASS ) )     ; A LIST of a lisp-number, a atom, and a list.
```

Figure 6.10: Output generated in the examples-only mode of a list description.

```
(LIST-MAIN-FEATURES
    LIST (LEFT-PARENTHESIS
            (KLEENE-CLOSURE DATA-ELEMENT)
            RIGHT-PARENTHESIS))

(DESCRIBE-FEATURE LEFT-PARENTHESIS LIST)
(DESCRIBE-FEATURE (KLEENE-CLOSURE DATA-ELEMENT) LIST)
(DESCRIBE-FEATURE RIGHT-PARENTHESIS LIST)
```

The planner searches for appropriate operators to satisfy the first of these goals. The operator to describe a list of features indicates that the features should be mentioned in a sequence. Three goals are appropriately posted at this point. These goals result in the planner generating a plan for describing the main features of a list: the left parenthesis, the data elements, and the right parenthesis. At this point, the portion of the discourse tree that has been constructed is identical to the one that was constructed for the top level NUCLEUS goal in the purely textual description that was presented in section 6.1. The discourse tree contains the structure and information necessary to generate the first sentence of the description: *"A list consists of a left parenthesis, zero or ... "*. A skeleton of the resulting text plan is shown in figure 6.6.

The system needs to expand the three SATELLITE goals to describe each of the three components of a list. As in the previous case, described in section 6.1, two of these SATELLITE goals, the ones to elaborate on the left and the right parentheses, founder for lack of additional information. Being *optional*, the system continues without trying to backtrack up a level.

The system now attempts to satisfy the goal

```
DESCRIBE-DATA-ELEMENTS
```

by finding an appropriate plan. Data elements can be of three types: numbers, symbols, or lists. The system can either communicate this information by realizing an appropriate sentence, or through examples (or both). The system is now no longer constrained to generate purely textual descriptions, as in section 6.1. Since the text is an introductory one, and the definition of a list has already been presented, heuristics in the system cause it to select examples for presentation. The introductory text type specifies that if a concept definition has been presented, elaborations are preferably realized in the form of examples immediately following the definition. The system therefore attempts to generate examples of a list which illustrate these different types of data elements. Since data elements can vary in two dimensions, it generates two goals, one for each dimension: the number of elements, and the type of different elements. The goal to illustrate the variable number of data elements causes the posting of two goals, one to generate an example with a single element, and one to generate an example with multiple (four) elements.

```
(GENERATE-EXAMPLE (VAR-FTR DATA-ELEMENT) 1 LIST)
(GENERATE-EXAMPLE (VAR-FTR DATA-ELEMENT) 4 LIST)
```

Note that the system picks the numbers 1 and 4 for the following reasons: the system needs to pick an example at the lower end of the range of possible numbers, and selects zero, but a list with no elements is defined as the symbol NIL as well. Since the symbol NIL classifies as an anomalous example, and this is an introductory text, the system decides to present one element as a data-element (one extreme of the number dimension is set to 1). At the other end of the range, the system picks 4 data-elements as the higher limit (the number 4 is hard coded into the system, based partially on the empirical observations by Clark (1971) that the most commonly seen number of examples in school settings was four). Both of these goals cause other goals to be posted to actually construct the example. The example generation algorithm ensures that (a) the examples selected for related subgoals (such as the two above) differ in only the dimension being highlighted; (b) the remaining dimensions are kept as simple as possible: thus the examples generated contain only atoms. (Both numbers and atoms are considered to be equally complex in this implementation, and numbers could also have been chosen to construct the three simpler lists; however, the implementation in LOOM returns the first of the retrieved list, and this happens, in this case, to be the concept atom.) The resulting output of these two goals is the presentation of two lists of atoms, one with a single element, and another with four elements.

Similarly, the goal to illustrate the type variability of elements in a list causes the generation of multiple goals: a goal to illustrate the fact that data elements can be atoms, numbers, number+atoms, lists, numbers+lists, and so on. The fact that there exists a kleene-closure of the data-elements causes the system to generate a power-set of all the sub-types. The set is then sorted in order of increasing complexity of the elements, using the top-level function ORDER-BY-COMPLEXITY. This computation of complexity is based on the algorithm described in section 5.3.5. The first four goals to present examples are selected. This is based on Clark's (1971) Maxim of Four Examples. The four goals are:

```
(GENERATE-EXAMPLE (VAR-FTR ATOM) LIST)

(GENERATE-EXAMPLE (VAR-FTR NUMBER) LIST)

(GENERATE-EXAMPLE (VAR-FTR (ATOM NUMBER)) LIST)

(GENERATE-EXAMPLE (VAR-FTR LIST)) LIST)
```

The first three goals are further expanded by posting appropriate goals to construct and present appropriate examples. However, in the fourth case, the text type prevents the system from simply generating an example of a list which has other lists as its data elements. This is because in introductory cases, the system cannot simply present examples of either recursive or anomalous cases without explicitly marking them as such: this is done through the presentation of information explaining such concepts to the user. The system therefore posts two goals, one to provide background information (which presents three simple lists), and the other to build a list from these three lists. The system needs to present three simple lists (three is chosen as a number between 1 and 4, the two limits in our system): these lists need to be simple, and therefore the previously presented list-examples, varying in both their number of elements as well as their type, are not selected for re-use. Presentations of recursive examples can either be annotated by prompts, or as in this case, accompanied (usually prefaced) with additional textual explanations. In the case of introductory texts, the system has the option of generating text (for advanced texts, however the system would be constrained from generating additional text, and would therefore generate prompts).

The resulting discourse structure is shown in figure 6.11.[9] The discourse structure is processed by the sentence realizer to an intermediate form, which represents only the speech acts and the rhetorical relations between them. This is shown in figure 6.13. The resulting English output is shown in figure 6.14.

---

[9] A simplified version of the text plan with communicative goals is shown in figure 6.12.

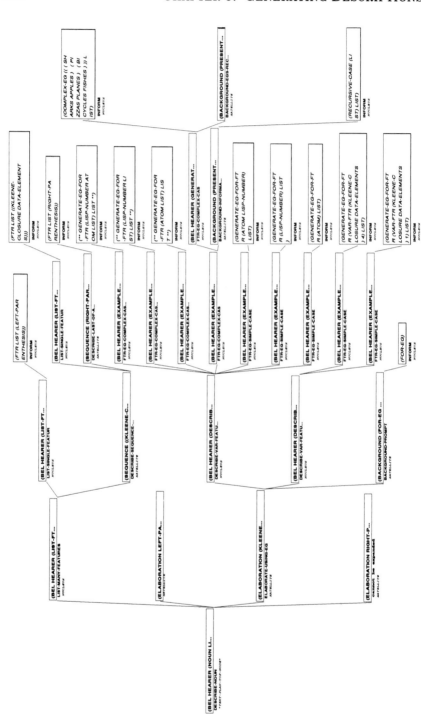

Figure 6.11: Text plan for a description of list with both text and examples.

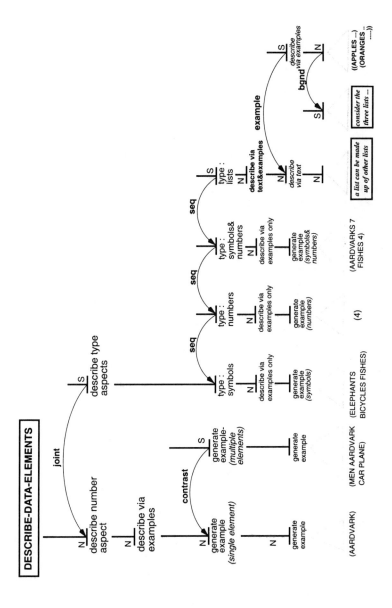

Figure 6.12: Part of the generated text plan for elaborating on the data-elements of a list.

```
(elaboration
 (sequence
  ((ftr list (left-parenthesis)))
  (sequence
   ((ftr list ((kleene-closure data-elements))))
   ((ftr list (right-parenthesis)))))
 (background
  ((for-eg))
  (((generate-eg-for-ftr
     (:var-ftr (kleene-closure data-elements) 1) list))
   ((generate-eg-for-ftr
     (:var-ftr (kleene-closure data-elements) 4) list)))
  (((generate-eg-for-ftr (atom) list))
   ((generate-eg-for-ftr (lisp-number) list))
   ((generate-eg-for-ftr (atom lisp-number) list))
  (background
   ((recursive-case (list) list))
   (background
    ((simple-egs
      (example-list-orange-orange-1
       example-list-aardvarks-elephants-2
       example-list-fishes-apples-11)
     list))
    (complex-eg
     ((example-list-orange-orange-1
       example-list-aardvarks-elephants-2
       example-list-fishes-apples-11))
     list))))))
```

Figure 6.13: Intermediate form used by the sentence realizer in generating the integrated description.

Paraphrase

DELETE BURY ROTATE

A list consists of a left parenthesis followed by
zero or more data elements followed by
a right parenthesis.   for example:

(FISHES)
(PLANES ORANGES PIZZAS PIZZAS)
(MONKEYS PLANES)
(1 3)
(MONKEYS 5 FISHES 2)

A list can also be made up of other lists.
Consider the 3 lists:

(ORANGES ORANGES)
(AARDVARKS ELEPHANTS)
(FISHES APPLES)

These can be used to form the list
((ORANGES ORANGES)   (AARDVARKS ELEPHANTS)   (FISHES APPLES)).

Figure 6.14: Output generated in the text-and-examples mode of a list's description.

6.4 Discussion

In this chapter, we have presented traces of the system in three different operating modes so as to clarify the working of the system. These
traces illustrate the integration between text and examples discussed
earlier in the book. The generation of the integrated description illustrates:

- Examples can replace textual explanations. The sentence describing the different types of data elements possible is replaced by examples illustrating the different types. This results in the elision
  of text.

- Examples can cause additional text to be generated; when anomalous or exceptional examples are presented, background text is
  added to introduce them. For example, the recursive example of
  a list of lists is prefaced with additional information.

The description in this chapter also illustrated two issues mentioned
previously; the ordering of features and examples by complexity, and
the selection of certain parameters so as not to present anomalous examples with the other regular examples (the system chose 1 rather
than 0 as the minimum number of elements in a list to avoid having to
present the anomalous case of NIL.) In the next chapter, we discuss the
generation of documentation for a more complex concept; this will help
illustrate some other conditions where additional textual explanations
are necessary if examples are presented.

Chapter 7

Negative Examples and Their Effect on Explanations

Technical Prose is almost immortal.

– Frederick P. Brooks, Jr.
The Mythical Man-Month

The previous chapter presented three different modes in which our system can generate concept descriptions illustrating how the presentation of examples can cause the elision of some text from the descriptive explanation, and how the presence of difficult (either recursive or anomalous) examples can require additional text to be presented with the example. In this chapter, we discuss the presentation of negative examples and how they affect the surrounding text. As we have already mentioned (section 3.6), negative examples are very useful in helping to convey the critical features of the concept. In this chapter, we illustrate how the system handles the issue of negative examples by generating documentation for concepts from the INTEND grammar (used in EES).

7.1   An Example from INTEND

The INTEND grammar used in EES is large and complex, with 125 productions, 21 filter functions and 91 terminal symbols. Many of these
productions are seemingly identical. This is because while the BNF
specifications of the syntax are the same, the filter functions test for different properties. For instance, consider the grammar productions for
a predicate-relation-form and a function-form shown in figure 7.1. Thus, with a grammar such as INTEND, it is important that the
documentation generated for a concept take into account other concepts
that are very similar to the one being described, and contrast them for
the reader. Productions such as these, represent patterns which can
be very effectively contrasted by using examples (Pólya, 1973). The
introduction of contrasting examples can result in the generation of
additional explanation. We will illustrate this aspect of the tight interaction between text and examples in this chapter.

One possible explanation generated by the system for the production
defining a predicate-form — whose BNF definition is given in figure 7.1 — is shown in figure 7.2. Consider the examples and the textual
explanation generated by the system. There are four examples presented in the explanation, three of which are positive, and the fourth is
negative. The negative example serves to highlight the differences between two closely related forms: a predicate-relation-form and
a function-form. Because the problem solving domain in question
happened to be that of local area networks, all of the examples that the
system constructed are from that domain. As in the scenario presented
in section 6.3, the interaction of the text and the examples can be seen
in various places:

1. the examples illustrate features mentioned in the text, namely
   the syntax of the predicate-relation-form

2. to make sure the first three examples are understood as positive
   examples, the system generates appropriate background text to
   introduce the examples: "Examples of predicate-relation-forms
   are ... "

3. the sentence "However, the following is not a (positive example)
   ... " is generated to explicitly highlight the contrast between positive and negative examples

```
if-form := '( 'IF predicate-form 'THEN expression
            { 'ELSE expression } ') ;

restricted-expression := var-name   | concept-desc  |
                function-form  | predicate-form ;

predicate-form := pred-relation-form  |
            pred-logical-form  | pred-action-form ;

pred-relation-form  :=
      '( relation-name restricted-expression + ')
        |>   pred-relation-form-test ;

pred-action-form := action-form    |> pred-action-test ;

pred-logical-form :=
    '( 'AND predicate-form + ')  |
    '( 'OR  predicate-form + ')  |
    '( 'NOT predicate-form ');

function-form  :=
      '( relation-name restricted-expression + ')
        |>   function-relation-form-test ;
```

Figure 7.1: A fragment of the INTEND grammar for EES.

A predicate-form is a restricted-expression. It returns a boolean value, and the number of arguments in a predicate-form is equal to the arity of the relation. A predicate-form can be of three types: a predicate-relation-form, a predicate-action-form, or a predicate-logical-form.

A predicate-relation-form consists of a relation-name followed by some arguments. The arguments are restricted-expressions, such as variables, concepts, function-forms and predicate-forms. Examples of predicate-relation-forms are:

```
(INDICATOR-STATE LED-1        ON)
(HARDWARE-STATUS LANBRIDGE-2 FAULTY)
(CONNECTED-TO    DECSERVER-1 VAX-A)
```

However, the following example is not a predicate-relation-form, but a function-form, because the number of arguments is not equal to the arity of the relation:

```
(CONNECTED-TO DECSERVER-1)
```

The difference between a function-form and a predicate-relation-form is that the function-form takes one less argument than the arity of the relation, and returns the range of the relation, while the predicate-logical-form takes as many arguments as the arity and returns a boolean value.

A predicate-action-form is ...

Figure 7.2: The documentation for `predicate-form`.

4. the negative example selected causes the generation of additional text both *before* and *after* the presentation of the example. This is because the example in question can fulfill two roles: it is not just *not a* `predicate-relation-form`, (and can thus be a negative example for that concept), but it is *also* a `function-form`, (and can therefore be a positive example for the latter). The `function-form` is a different, but similar construct that can be contrasted with the `predicate-relation-form`. Additional text is generated first to introduce the negative example as a contrast to the positive ones, and later to explain the differences between the two similar constructs.

This scenario also illustrates the other aspects that have to be taken into consideration when generating integrated text and examples:

- *Fixed Features:* As previously mentioned in section 3.6, it is important for the system to differentiate between *variable features* and *critical features* because of the differences in the way examples are presented to illustrate them. It is also useful for the system to represent and reason about *fixed features*. Fixed features are critical features representing terminal symbols that are specified as being known to the user.[12] For instance, terminal symbols such as the keywords "defun" and "defmacro" in the LISP domain may be specified as fixed features once the system has presented definitions and examples of functions and macros to the user. After these keywords (critical features in the examples) have been annotated in the system as being 'fixed', the system will:

  - not explicitly mention these features in its textual explanation when explaining either the same concept or its subconcepts;
  - not generate negative examples for these features.

  For instance, if the system is generating examples of functions to calculate, for instance, the factorial of a number, the system will

---

[1]This also satisfies Grice's *Second Maxim of Conciseness* by omitting facts that are already known to the user.

[2]Also helps the system avoid the *Penguin Syndrome*, so named because an incident a few years ago, when a publisher of childrens' books had one of their books about penguins returned in the mail. The returned book was accompanied by the following note in a young child's scrawl: *"Dear Sirs: I am returning your book because it told me more about penguins than I wanted to know."* (Morgan, 1980).

not generate negative examples of functions that do not have the keyword "defun;" instead the negative examples would be concerned with other aspects of the functional specification. Fixed features are dependent on the context (what has been presented earlier, or what is represented in the user model), and are used to prevent the system from generating overly verbose explanations. In this scenario, the fact that a `predicate-relation-form` is specified to begin and end with a parenthesis is considered by the system to be an instance of a fixed feature. Thus, the parentheses are not mentioned in the accompanying explanation, nor does the system generate negative examples with missing parentheses.

Variable features are those which can vary within a certain range in a positive example — in this case, the `relation-name` is a variable feature. It is usually necessary to provide several examples to communicate the variable nature of the feature (Clark, 1971). In this case, several different relation-names are used in an attempt to ensure that the user realizes its variable nature.

Critical features are features that, if modified, cause the example to change from positive to negative. Critical features in this case are the number of arguments that follow the `relation-name`; there must be exactly as many arguments as the arity of the relation.

- *Presentation Order:* The presentation order of the examples depends on the complexity of the features they illustrate; the ordering is also important to communicate the critical features of a concept (as discussed in section 3.6). In this case, the variable features and the critical features both require two examples; since the negative example of the second pair is an "interesting" negative example (resulting in more explanations), the examples illustrating the variable feature are presented before the second pair.

- *Additional Explanation:* text to draw attention to specific points in the examples might be needed to render explicit the implicit information that may otherwise be overlooked. In this case, the need to introduce the positive and negative examples is quite clear; however, the information on the negative example being a `function-form` could have been easily overlooked.

This scenario illustrates again the close relationship between text and examples. The next section describes how our generation system can generate such explanations.

7.2 Plan Operators

Two of the plan operators used in this example are shown in figure 7.3.[3] As mentioned earlier, the constraints of the plan operators indicate how the text and the examples co-constrain each other.

The first plan operator can be used to describe a concept and one of its role restrictions, e.g., it could be used to describe the fact that a `predicateform` is constrained to return a BOOLEAN value. The first constraint finds the type of the role restriction on the concept (whether its a value restriction — as in the case of the BOOLEAN, or whether its a number restriction, and so on). This is necessary because the eventual phrasing depends upon this information. The second constraint finds all the features pertaining to this role and the concept that need to be presented, taking into account the user model and the previous discourse. The next constraint determines the features that can be presented in the form of examples: this is dependent upon both the features themselves — syntactic features can be expressed through examples, but not structural features — as well as the explanation context — whether for instance, the appropriate definition has already been presented. The last constraint filters out the fixed features that the planner should not present in text. At this point, the operator can be selected, since all of its constraints have been satisfied. It therefore posts two subgoals: one to present a textual explanation of the role restriction on the concept, and another, optional subgoal, to present examples of the concept that illustrate the role restriction.

The second plan operator can be used to present a contrasting pair of positive–negative examples. The first constraint finds a positive example for the concept illustrating the role. The second constraint finds a negative example by using the same information, as well as the positive example constructed as a result of the previous constraint being satisfied. The third constraint checks to see whether the negative example

---

[3]As explained previously, the plan operators shown here have been simplified somewhat; for instance, the constraints that take into account the text type have been removed from these two operators for the sake of brevity.

constructed is an interesting one or not. If all of these constraints are satisfied, the planner can apply this operator. This results in the planner posting three sub-goals: one to present the positive example and two for the negative example. The two sub-goals for the negative example result in the background text ("However, this is not a ... ") and the actual example and the differences.[4]

7.3 Describing Predicate-Relation-Form

The system initially begins with the top-level goal of:

    (BEL HEARER (CONCEPT PREDICATE-FORM))

The text planner searches for applicable plan operators in its plan-library, and, finding an applicable plan operator,[5] it posts two subgoals: one to give a definition of the concept (predicate-form), and another (optional one) to elaborate upon this definition. (This is the same plan operator that was utilized by the planner for generating the descriptions of a list in sections 6.1 and 6.3.) At this point then, the planner has two goals:[6]

    (DESCRIBE (CONCEPT PREDICATE-FORM))
    (ELABORATE PREDICATE-FORM)

The planner expands the first subgoal by providing a definition of the concept predicate-form. There are a number of different ways in which a concept definition can be provided. For instance, a concept can be defined in terms of its parent with their differentiating attributes clearly specified. Another way would be to present its syntactic or structural description, as was done in the case of the list. Yet another way is to describe the concept in terms of its disjoint coverings (such as describing people as being either males or females). The method used

---

[4]While many classical theorists in rhetoric have agreed on the uses of positive examples, relatively few have suggested that negative ones may also be useful. Virgil was one of the exceptions and suggested that both positive and negative examples should be presented. As discussed earlier, the Direct Instruction Model stresses the importance of not just positive and negative ones, but also the contrast between the two.

[5]There are several plans available in the plan library for describing objects. The system chooses one using *selection heuristics* designed by Moore (1989).

[6]As in the previous chapter, we shall not use the formal notation in presenting goals for the sake of clarity.

```
(define-text-plan-operator
  :EFFECT (BEL HEARER (ref (def-attr ?concept) ?role))
  :CONSTRAINTS
   (and
     (get-restriction-type ?restriction-type ?role ?concept)
     (get-ftrs ?features ?role ?concept *user-model*
                               *explanation-context*)
     (get-eg-ftrs ?ftrs-only-in-eg ?features ?role
          ?concept *user-model* *explanation-context*)
     (filter-fixed-ftrs ?features-in-text ?features
       ?ftrs-only-in-eg *user-model* *explanation-context*)))
  :NUCLEUS
     (INFORM S hearer
        (?restriction-type ?role ?ftrs-in-text))
  :SATELLITES
     (((ELABORATION-BY-EXAMPLE
        ?features ?role ?concept) *optional*)))
```

```
(define-text-plan-operator
  :EFFECT (EXAMPLE ?ftrs ?concept ?role))
  :CONSTRAINTS
    (and
      (get-pos-eg ?pos-eg ?ftrs ?concept ?role)
      (get-neg-eg ?neg-eg ?pos-eg ?ftrs ?concept
                               ?role-restricted)
      (significant-neg-example? ?new-concept ?neg-eg))
  :NUCLEUS
     (BEL HEARER (example ?pos-eg ?ftrs ?concept ?role))
  :SATELLITES
     (((BACKGROUND
        (neg-example ?neg-eg ?concept ?role)) *optional*)
      ((EVIDENCE
        (counter-example ?neg-eg ?ftrs ?new-concept ?role))
                               *optional*)))
```

Figure 7.3: Two sample text planning operators that can be used to present negative examples.

to describe the concept depends upon the concept: for instance, in the case of `list`, the parent concept of the `list` was `grammar-symbol`. Because a `grammar-symbol` is any symbol in the grammar, the system did not describe a list as being a grammar-symbol. In the case of a `predicate-form`, the system does not have the option of presenting the syntactic definition, because it does not have a syntactic definition. The system could present a description of the `predicate-form` in terms of its sub-types, but the selection heuristics pick the first method (describing it in terms of its parent) over the third method (in terms of its children). This results in the first two sentences of the explanation:

> A `predicate-form` is a `restricted-expression`. It returns a boolean value, and the number of arguments is equal to the arity of the relation.

The SATELLITE goal to elaborate upon a `predicate-form` is now expanded by the planner. The only information that the system has about the `predicate-form` that has not been expressed is that the concept `predicate-form` can be of three types:

1. `predicate-relation-forms`

2. `predicate-action-forms`, and

3. `predicate-logical-forms`.

The planner expands the satellite goal by posting two goals: one to present this information about the three sub-types, and another to describe each of the three sub-types. The NUCLEUS sub-goal is a primitive goal which results in the generation of the third sentence in the documentation:

> A `predicate-form` can be one of three types: a predicate-relation-form, a predicateaction-form, or a predicate-logical-form.

The goals to elaborate upon each sub-type of a `predicate-form` will be expanded in turn. Because these sub-types might be of differing complexity, and it is important to present the information from

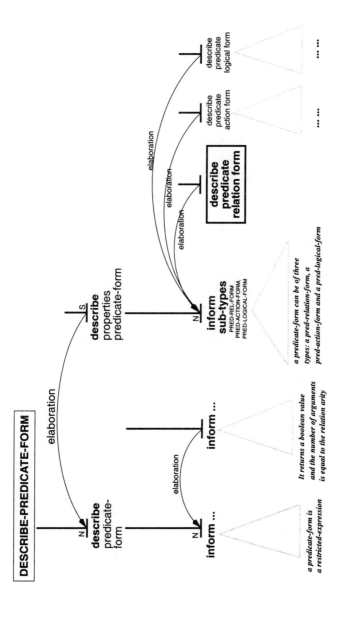

Figure 7.4: A skeletal fragment of the text plan generated for the initial text.

the simplest one to the most complex one[7] The resulting ordering is: `predicate-relation-form` followed by `predicate-action-form` followed by `predicate-logical-form`. Each elaboration results in posting the goal of describing a sub-type. So the three sub-goals are posted in turn.

```
(ELABORATE (CONCEPT-DESCRIPTION PREDICATE-RELATION-FORM)
(ELABORATE (CONCEPT-DESCRIPTION PREDICATE-ACTION-FORM))
(ELABORATE (CONCEPT-DESCRIPTION PREDICATE-LOGICAL-FORM)
```

This portion of the planning process is recorded in the skeleton text-plan shown in figure 7.4. This text plan shows the communicative goals that have been posted as well as the coherence relations between them.

The first goal that the planner expands is the one to describe the concept `predicate-relation-form`. As in the case of `predicate-form`, the system has a number of options that it can use to describe it. The first option is to describe it in terms of its parent concept: a `predicate-form`. This is not chosen because the concept-parent relationship between a `predicate-relation-form` and a `predicate-form` has already been mentioned previously. (The `predicate-relation-form` was introduced as a sub-type of `predicate-form`.) The second option of describing a concept in terms of its syntax is applicable in this case, because there is a syntactic definition associated with the concept. The third option of describing the concept in terms of its sub-types is not applicable in this case. Thus, the planner selects the plan operator that describes the syntax of the concept. In this case, the syntax is:

```
PREDICATE-RELATION-FORM := ' ( RELATION-NAME {ARGUMENT +} ' )
```

Instantiating the plan operator, the system has the option of describing the syntax in textual form, or through examples (since the text type is introductory, the system can present examples at any point). However, the system has not yet presented a definition of `predicate-relation-form`. In introductory texts examples can be presented only after the definition of the concept. The plan operator chosen by the system posts two sub-goals: one to present the definition (in text), and the other to elaborate upon `predicate-relation-form` through examples.

---

[7]As mentioned in section 3.6, one of the constraints in the plan operator selected explicitly orders the sub-types using the function ORDER-BY-COMPLEXITY, before posting the sub-goals to describe them in turn.

```
(PRESENT (CONCEPT-DEFINITION PREDICATE-RELATION-FORM))
(ELABORATE (CONCEPT-DEFINITION PREDICATE-RELATION-FORM))
```

Before the two sub-goals are posted, the constraints of the plan operator selected compute the parameters that determine what gets expressed via text, via examples and both. The plan operator in this case is very similar to the first plan operator in figure 7.3. In the case of the `predicate-relation-form`, the system determines[8] that there are three critical features, i.e., the left parenthesis, the right parenthesis, and the number of arguments in the `predicate-relation-form` (which must be equal to the arity of the relation). There is only one variable feature: the parameter `relation-name`, which is the name assigned to the relation. The arguments to the name of the relation are constrained by the relation chosen, so they are not independently variable. The system also determines that the parentheses should not be mentioned in the text as they are fixed features, and will be mentioned in all the examples.

The system now has enough information to continue with the presentation planning process: the first sub-goal posted, to present the definition of the concept expands into two sub-goals:

```
(INFORM S HEARER (ISA RELATION-NAME PREDICATE-RELATION-FORM))
(SEQUENCE (SYNTAX-FTRS ARGUMENTS PREDICATE-RELATION-FORM))
```

The first sub-goal results in:

> *A predicate-relation-form consists of a relation-name.*

The coherence relation SEQUENCE between the two goals causes the generation of the cue phrase *followed by*, and the second sub-goal results in *A predicate-relation-form has some arguments*. When these two sub-goals, along with the coherence relation, are processed by the sentence generator, it results in:

> A predicate-relation-form consists of a relation name followed by some arguments.

The sub-goal to describe the arguments also causes the posting of a

---

[8]As described in section 5.3.2, the system determines critical features and variable features by modifying the definitions and seeing whether an example of the modified definition becomes a negative example of the concept, using the LOOM classifier.

goal to elaborate upon the fact that `restricted-expressions` can be
of different types such as variables, concepts, and function-forms. This
is realized by a primitive speech act as shown in figure 7.5. Thus, the
planner has generated the first four sentences at this point.

The planner now has to expand the goal of:

```
(ELABORATE (CONCEPT-DEFINITION
                PREDICATE-RELATION-FORM))
```

At this point the definition of a `predicate-relation-form` has already been presented, and the system can present examples of a

```
    PREDICATE-RELATION-FORM
```

to satisfy this goal. As described in section 5.3.2, the variable and critical features computed previously are retrieved. During the computation of the critical features, the system modifies the definition of the
`predicate-relation-form` by reducing the number of arguments by
one (as described in the algorithm in section 5.3.2). An example generated for this modified definition classifies under the concept `function-
form`. Because the system finds an interesting negative example, it
orders the other examples so that the negative example is presented
last (according to the ordering criteria given in section 5.3.5). The
system needs to present at least two examples to illustrate a variable feature. These two examples illustrating the variable feature (the
`relation-name`) are to be presented first, followed by the pair for the
critical features. The planner must also indicate that the examples are
positive and negative as well. This is done through the posting of a
BACKGROUND goal to generate text to introduce the positive examples.
This is followed by a goal to generate the examples for the variable features, and the goal to generate examples for the critical feature. Since
examples illustrating variable features should be widely different, the
system generates examples with two different relations, and the first
two examples are generated. This part of the text plan is shown in
figure 7.5.

In the case of the positive–negative pair to illustrate the critical feature, the positive example can be presented without any introduction
because the immediately preceding examples are positive examples as
well. To present the negative example, the system must generate additional introductory text to explicitly mark the example as being negative. The planner posts an appropriate goal to generate text to intro-

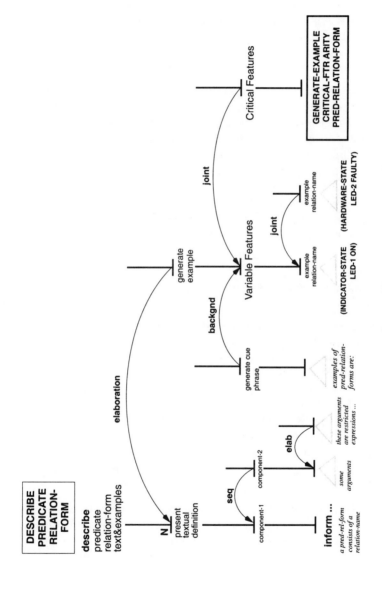

Figure 7.5: Plan fragment for the predicate-relation-form.

duce the negative example. This is linked to the goal for presenting the positive example with the coherence relation CONTRAST. This results in the generation of a cue phrase such as "However, ..." The presentation of the negative example is accompanied by the presentation of a goal to elaborate upon the differences between a predicate-relation-form and a function-form. The relevant portions of the text-plan are shown in figure 7.6.

The planner continues expanding goals in this fashion, until all the goals are primitive speech-acts, such as (INFORM ...). Finally, the completed discourse tree is passed to an interface that converts the INFORM goals into the appropriate input for the sentence generator. The interface constructs the individual sentences as well as connects them appropriately, using the rhetorical information from the discourse tree. For example, it chooses "However" to reflect the CONTRAST relation. It also chooses the appropriate lexical items. Finally, the sentence generator produces the English. The resulting output is shown in figures 7.7 and 7.8.

7.4   Discussion

In this chapter, we have seen additional ways in which both examples and text interact with and co-constrain each other. It is important to recognize and present interesting negative examples when they are available; however, such examples can cause additional text to be generated, as well as affect the order in which the examples are to be presented. It is important to recognize this interaction in order to provide an appropriate, well-structured, and coherent presentation to the user. This chapter has reinforced the argument that example generation must be considered as an integral part of the generation process. Our scenario from the documentation system has illustrated some of these issues.

In the next chapter, we look at the effect of the text type on the generation process, and study the major differences between the descriptions that occur in introductory versus advanced texts.

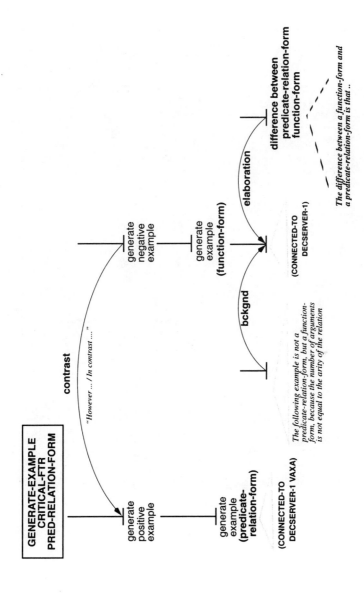

Figure 7.6: Text-plan fragment for the generation of the examples for the critical feature.

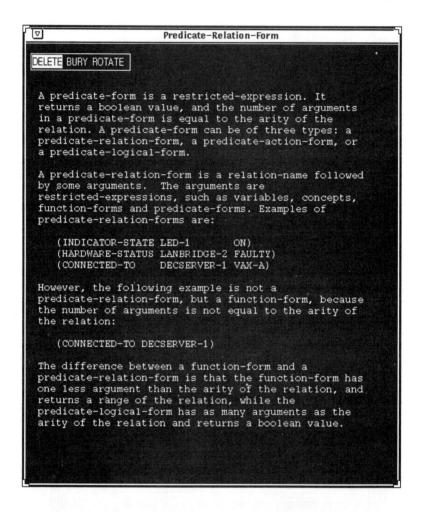

Figure 7.7: Documentation for `predicate-relation-form` with examples.

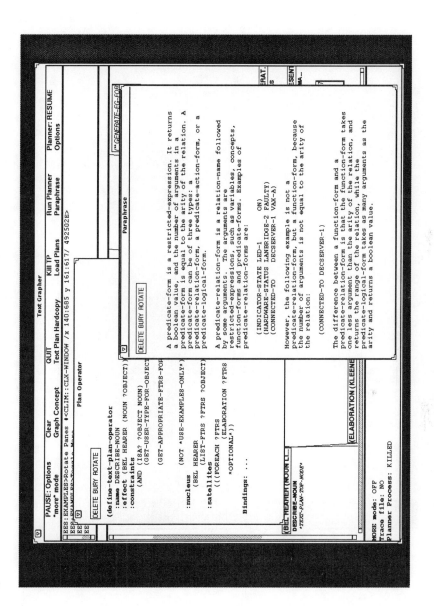

Figure 7.8: A snapshot of the system generating documentation.

Chapter 8

The Effect of the Text Type on Descriptions

The previous chapters discussed two instances of the interaction between the text and the examples: the elision of text due to the presentation of 'equivalent' examples, and the addition of text, due to the presence of anomalous, or negative examples. All of the previous descriptions have been generated for an introductory text type. Given another text type, the descriptions can be very different. It is important to generate appropriate descriptions in different situations. This chapter analyzes the differences between introductory, intermediate, and advanced text types. While we shall discuss the main points of each of these three text types, it must be emphasized that our implementation as yet does not have a representation for the intermediate text type. Thus, our generation can only be done for the introductory and advanced text types. This is because we do not, as yet, represent the semantics of the various constructs, and these are essential in the generation of descriptions for intermediate texts. This chapter presents the main differences between these three types, describes how introductory and advanced texts affect the generation of concept descriptions. We have already seen the generation of a list for an introductory text; in this chapter, we shall trace the generation of a description for an advanced text to contrast the two processes and thus illustrate our points.

A list always begins with a left parenthesis. Then come zero or more pieces of data (called the elements of a list) and a right parenthesis. Some examples of lists are:

```
(AARDVARK)
(RED YELLOW GREEN BLUE)
(2 3 5 11 19)
(3 FRENCH FRIES)
```

A list may contain other lists as elements. Given the three lists:

```
(BLUE SKY)  (GREEN GRASS)  (BROWN EARTH)
```

we can make a list by combining them all with a parentheses.

```
((BLUE SKY)  (GREEN GRASS)  (BROWN EARTH))
```

From (Touretzky, 1984), p. 35.

Figure 8.1: A description of `list` in an introductory text.

First we discuss the need to vary the descriptions. Then we describe what a text type is considered to be, and its implications for the text as well as the examples. We later deal with each of the effects, and describe how one of the differences noticed in our corpus — the placement of the examples with respect to the text — can be explained by using the text type. Finally, the rest of the chapter traces the generation of the advanced text scenario to show how these issues are considered in this implementation.

8.1 The Need to Vary Descriptions

Different situations can result in widely varying descriptions. The variation can occur in both the textual descriptions and the accompanying examples. Contrast the two descriptions for the same concept — a list — given in figures 8.1 and 8.2. Not only is the textual description different, the examples — in terms of number, content, position, etc. — are different as well. It is therefore essential to generate descriptions which take into account the situation. In this case, we are concerned

A list is recursively defined to be either the empty list or a CONS whose CDR component is a list. The CAR components of the CONSes are called the elements of the list. For each element of the list, there is a CONS. The empty list has no elements at all.

A list is annotated by writing the elements of the list in order, separated by blank space (space, tab, or return character) and surrounded by parentheses. For example:

```
(a b c)                    ; A list of 3 symbols
(2.0s0 (a 1) #\*)          ; A list of 3 things:a
                           ; floating point number,
                           ; another list, and a
                           ; character object
```

From (Steele Jr., 1984), p. 26.

Figure 8.2: A description of list from a reference manual.

with generating descriptions in different text types.

A number of researchers have studied the effects of different situations on the textual description: for example, Paris (1988) and Paris and Bateman (1989) studied the changes resulting in the text based on the intended user (a concept analogous to the text type). Polya (1945) and Michener (1978) presented characterizations of different example types. However, there has been no work on the characterization of *descriptions that include examples* in different text types.

One cannot independently plan a description tailored to a user, separately generate examples tailored to the user, and then present them together: Sweller et al. found that if the examples and the descriptive component were not integrated, the combination could result in reduced user comprehension (Chandler and Sweller, 1991; Ward and Sweller, 1990). Examples and text must be presented to the user as a coherent whole, and together, appropriately tailored to the situation. Yet, the issue of tailoring descriptions that include examples for the situation at hand has not been addressed.

8.2   The Notion of a Text Type

It has long been observed that certain types of linguistic phenomena such as the rhetorical structure, lexical types, grammatical features, and others closely reflect the genre of the text, such as introductory tutorial material, reference manuals, etc. Several text typologies have been proposed by linguists. For instance, Biber (1989) identified eight basic types of texts based on statistically derived grammatical patterns and lexical commonalities; the Washington School proposed a detailed classification of different genres of written scientific and technical English (Trimble, 1985), and de Beaugrande (1980) proposed a general classification of text types, arguing that text types determine the types of discourse structure relations used.

A text generation system can make use of the notion of text types to constrain its options, such as which communicative goals to achieve, which discourse relations to favor, any appropriate grammatical constraints, etc. In our case, text types play a particularly important role in the generation of examples and their positioning. More specifically, for descriptions, two text types — *introductory* and *advanced* — constrain the positioning of examples with respect to the descriptive material. These are the two text types that we describe in this chapter and are used by the implemented system.

8.3   Integrating Examples: Issues Related to the Text Type

Many issues need to be considered when generating descriptions that integrate descriptive text and examples, because both these components co-constrain and affect each other. While we have discussed these issues in previous chapters, especially chapter 3, we review some of them here:

- What should be in the text, in the examples, in both?

- What is a suitable example? How much information should a single example attempt to convey? Should there be more than one example?

- If multiple examples are to be presented, what is the order of presentation?

- If an example is to be given, should the example be presented immediately, or after the whole description is presented?[1]

- Should prompts be generated along with the examples?

Answers to these questions depend on whether the text is an introductory or advanced text. Consider, for example, the descriptions of list given in figure 8.1 taken from (Touretzky, 1984), an introductory book, and figure 8.2 taken from (Steele Jr., 1984), an advanced, reference book: they contain very different information in both their descriptive portions as well as their examples; while figure 8.1 contains eight lists (which are used either as examples or as background to the examples), figure 8.2 has only two lists as examples. The elements of the examples in the two descriptions are also significantly different: the numbers in figure 8.1 are integers, such as 2 and 3, while the number used as an element in figure 8.2 is a more complex instance: 2.0s0. The examples in figure 8.1 do not contain prompts, while those in figure 8.2 do. Finally, the examples appear very differently placed (with respect to the explanation) in the two figures.

The next section discusses each of these issues in turn.

8.4 Introductory vs. Advanced Texts

We now consider how descriptions that contain examples differ from introductory to advanced text. Note that this is one of the dimensions for example categorization that we described in chapter 4. We shall address each of the questions presented in section 8.3. The different components that can vary are:

- **The descriptive component:** in the case of the introductory texts, the descriptive component contains surface or syntactic information. This fact was found to be true in our entire corpus without exception; it was also noted in other studies as well, for

---

[1]This will determine whether the example(s) appear *within*, *before*, or *after* the descriptive text.

example, (MacLachlan, 1986; Charney, Reder, and Wells, 1988; Reder, Charney, and Morgan, 1986).

Reference material is technical, detailed and comprehensive. The material usually contains all the facts about the system (including the internal structure of the concept), forming the basis for all other types of documentation (Brockmann, 1986).

- **The actual examples:** examples in both text types illustrate critical features of the surface or syntactic form of the concept or its realization. In introductory texts, however, examples are simple and tend to illustrate only one feature at a time. (Sometimes it is not possible to isolate one feature, and an example might illustrate two features; in this case, the system will need to generate additional text — such as a prompt — to mention this fact.) On the other hand, examples in reference texts are multi-featured.

- **The number of examples**: since introductory texts contain usually single-featured examples, the number of examples depend upon the number of critical features that the concept possesses. In contrast, as reference texts contain examples that contain three or four features per example (Clark, 1971), proportionately fewer examples need to be presented.

- **The polarity of the examples:** introductory texts make use of both positive and negative examples, but not anomalous examples. Advanced texts on the other hand, contain positive and anomalous examples, but usually not negative ones.

- **The position of the examples**: in introductory texts, the examples are presented immediately after the point they illustrate is mentioned. This results in descriptions in which the examples are interspersed in the text. On the other hand, examples in reference texts must be presented only after the description of the concept is complete.

- **Prompts**: in general, prompts are generated when an example contains more than one feature. The system must also generate prompts in the case of recursive examples (these are examples that have as elements other examples of the concept), and anomalous examples if background text has not yet been generated. In introductory texts, background text is usually generated and thus prompts are not necessary. In contrast, in advanced texts, the examples are grouped at the end, after the textual description; background text cannot be generated at that point, so prompts may be necessary.

These observations are summarized in figure 8.3.

The six factors listed above are the major reasons for differences between introductory texts and advanced texts.[2] Taking these into account, our system can generate descriptions that match naturally occurring ones in the corpus. The role these factors play will be illustrated by working through the generation of descriptions similar to ones presented in figures 8.1 and 8.2.

Each of the factors described in the previous section affects some of the other factors in varying degrees. For instance, the number of examples is dependent upon the number of features presented in each of the examples; the presence of prompts depends upon the number of features and the number of examples, etc. However, one of these factors, the placement of the examples with respect to the text, is more important than the others. This is because this factor, *the positioning of the examples, directly affects all of the other five factors.* The next section describes the effect of the text type on the other factors.

8.5 Positioning the Examples

Examples can either occur *before* the text, *within* the text, or *after* the text. Consider for instance, the description in figures 8.4 and 8.5, taken from two introductory books, one on UNIX (Waite, Martin, and Prata, 1983), and the other on TEX (Abrahams, Berry, and Hargreaves, 1990). In both cases, the descriptions have examples interspersed *within* the text. Consider the descriptions given in figure 8.6 where the examples occur *before* the accompanying description, and figure 8.7 where the examples occur *after* the description.

The three descriptions of a list in LISP given in figure 8.8, illustrate three different descriptions occurring in three different text types. The placement of the examples in each of the descriptions is different: in

---

[2]These factors do not take into consideration differences in the phrasing and lexical choice.

For each issue, the effect of the text-type is:

- Examples:

  introductory: simple, single critical-feature

  advanced: complex, multiple critical-features

- Accompanying Description:

  introductory: surface, syntactic information

  advanced: complete information, including internal structure

- Number of Examples:

  introductory: depends upon number of critical features

  advanced: few (each example contains three to four features)

- Positioning the Examples:

  introductory: immediately after points being illustrated

  advanced: after the description is complete

- Prompts:

  introductory: prompt if example has more than one feature

  advanced: prompts if anomalous and recursive examples

Figure 8.3: Brief description of differences between examples in introductory and advanced texts.

UNIX has a **who** command, which results in a list of the people logged onto the system at that moment. An example of the command and its output is:

```
% who
bob             tty04 Aug 23  8:27
catfish         tty07 Aug 23  8:16
sneezy          tty15 Aug 23  8:52
granny          tty21 Aug 23 23:13
%
```

The first column gives the login name of the user. The second column identifies the terminal being used. The remaining columns give the date and time each user logged in.

From (Waite, Martin, and Prata, 1983), p. 50.

Figure 8.4: Introductory Text: Examples within the description (a).

A *delimiter* in TEX is a character that is intended to be used as a visible boundary of a math formula. For example, the left and right parentheses are delimiters. If delimiters are used around a formula, TEX makes the delimiters big enough to enclose the box that contains the formula. For example:

```
$$ \left( a \over b \right) $$
```

yields:

$$\left(\frac{a}{b}\right)$$

TEX made the parentheses big enough to accomodate the fraction. But, if instead of the previous expression, one had:

```
$$ ({a \over b})$$
```

the result would be:

$$(\frac{a}{b})$$

Since the parentheses are not in a delimiter context, they are *not* enlarged.

From (Abrahams, Berry, and Hargreaves, 1990), p. 58.

Figure 8.5: Introductory Text: Examples within the description (b).

Consider the following expression, in which + is followed by something other than raw numbers:

```
(+ (* 2 2) (/ 2 2))
```

It is easy to see that (* 2 2) produces 4, (/ 2 2) produces 1, and these results, fed in turn to +, give 5 as the result. If, instead, we think of this expression as data, then we see that we have the three element list: + is the first element, the expression (* 2 2) is the second element and (/ 2 2) is the third. Thus lists themselves can be part of other lists.

From (Winston and Horn, 1984), p. 20.

Figure 8.6: Intermediate Text: Examples before an explanation.

Used without arguments, **who** lists the login name, terminal name, and login time for each current user. who gets this information from the /etc/utmp file.

[... 16 lines deleted ...]

```
example% who am i
example!ralph  ttyp0      Apr 27 11:24
example%
example% who
mktg    ttym0   Apr 27 11:11
gwen    ttyp0   Apr 27 11:25
ralph   ttyp1   Apr 27 11:30
example%
```

From (UNIX Documentation, 1986)

Figure 8.7: Advanced Text: Examples after the description.

A list always begins with a left parenthesis. Then come zero or more pieces of
data (called the elements of a list) and a right parenthesis. Some examples of
lists are:

```
(AARDVARK)
(RED YELLOW GREEN BLUE)
(2 3 5 11 19)
(3 FRENCH FRIES)
```
A list may contain other lists as elements. Given the three lists:

```
(BLUE SKY) (GREEN GRASS) (BROWN EARTH)
```
we can make a list by combining them all with a parentheses.

```
((BLUE SKY) (GREEN GRASS) (BROWN EARTH))
```

Introductory text (Touretzky, 1984)

```
(FORMAT *standard-output* "~a~d~a"
        (name person) (age person)
        (if (> (age person) 65) "senior" () ))
```

A list can contain atoms, numbers, strings or other lists as elements. For
instance, the example above contains two atoms, a string and three lists as
elements. A list can have any number of elements, as in the example above,
where the top-level list contains six elements, and the some of the other lists
contain two, three and zero elements. A list can also be a function, if it can be
evaluated: in this case, the first element of the list is the name of the function.

Intermediate text (Winston and Horn, 1984)

A list is recursively defined to be either the empty list or a CONS whose CDR
component is a list. The CAR components of the CONSes are called the elements of the list. For each element of the list, there is a CONS. The empty
list has no elements at all. A list is annotated by writing the elements of the
list in order, separated by blank space (space, tab, or return character) and
surrounded by parentheses. For example:

```
(a b c)                  ;   a list of 3 symbols
(2.0s0 (a 1) #\*)        ;   a list of 3 things: a short floating point
                         ;   number, another list and a character object
```

Advanced text (Steele Jr., 1984)

Figure 8.8: Three descriptions of a list in different text types.

the introductory case, the examples are interspersed within the description, in the intermediate case, the examples are before the description, and in the advanced case, the examples are after the description. These descriptions of a list emphasize how the same object can be presented very differently in different situations. We have already presented the generation of a list for an introductory text previously; in this chapter, we shall generate a description for an advanced text to illustrate how the placement of the examples affects the resulting descriptions.

8.5.1 Effect of the Positioning on Comprehension

The position in which the examples appear affect the descriptions significantly. Studies on the efficacy of presenting examples in different positions with regard to the accompanying description showed that examples *within* and *after* the description are used most often. Klausmeier showed that texts for naive users were most effective when the example *immediately followed* the definition of the concept being illustrated (Klausmeier, 1976). Maclachlan (1986) found a number of correlations between the position of examples and their comprehension. His study found that the presentation of an example followed by an explanation of that example[3] (rather than an explanation of the concept that the example was an instance of) was an effective teaching method when the user was already familiar with the concept.[4] Most reference manuals include examples clustered *after* the description, as can be seen in, for instance, (Meehan, 1979; Lucid, 1990; Steele Jr., 1984; UNIX Documentation, 1986). It is clear therefore, that each of these three possibilities may occur during generation, and must be handled by the generation system.

8.5.2 Deciding Example Positions

Our corpus analysis has enabled us to identify two factors which govern the positioning of examples with respect to the description:

---

[3]Thus resulting in a description where the example appeared *before* the accompanying explanation.

[4]This method is most effective when the user possesses a declarative knowledge of the concept, but lacks sufficient procedural knowledge about it to use the knowledge to do something with it.

1. the *text type* in which the description is being generated, and

2. the *communicative goal* that the example achieves.

The notion of a text type has previously been discussed in this chapter. The communicative goal,[5] or intentional goal, represents a desired state of affairs for the system to achieve. Examples of such goals in our system are:

```
(BEL HEARER (CONCEPT LIST))
(BEL HEARER (DISJOINT-COVERING
            S-EXPRESSION (ATOM NUMBER STRING LIST)))
```

The first communicative goal, for instance, causes the system to present to the hearer a description of a `list`. The second generates a description of the fact that an `s-expression` has a disjoint-covering of either an `atom`, a `number`, a `string` or a `list`. Among the many advantages in representing the intentional goals explicitly in the discourse structure that is generated by the planner is the ability to recover from communication failures, to engage in dialogue, and answer follow-up questions (Moore and Paris, 1989; Moore and Swartout, 1989). Communicative goals are also essential in determining where an example should be positioned with respect to the accompanying explanation.

An algorithm to determine the placement of examples is shown in figure 8.9. The algorithm generates descriptions with examples that match the texts in our corpus, as well as the desiderata mentioned in psychological literature. For instance, examples should be presented after the definition in introductory texts (Feldman, 1972; Klausmeier, 1976); cases where the examples are the focus of instruction should have an elaboration on the features of the example rather than the concept, and so on.

The next section elaborates on the algorithm, and discusses the effects of the positioning on the five other factors that vary with the text type.

---

[5]Communicative goals have been mentioned previously in the context of our description of the system generating explanations. We briefly present it here, for the sake of completeness.

The decision to place an example before, within, or after the description depends on two co-constraining factors:

1. **The Text Type:**
   - if the text type is either tutorial or introductory, and appropriate examples are available, generate examples to illustrate points as soon as they are mentioned in the description (examples occur within the description)
   - if the text type is a reference text, prevent examples from being generated until the description is complete (examples appear after the description)

2. **The Communicative Goal:**
   - if the top-level communicative goal can be achieved through an example, and the text type does not prevent it, then present the example and elaborate upon it in the description. (example occurs *before* the elaboration in the description)
   - if a communicative goal, which is not a top-level communicative goal, can be realized through the presentation of examples, and the text type does not prevent it, then present the examples (*within* the description)
   - if the presentation of example(s) achieves a goal to elaborate on a concept, and this goal is posted after a goal (at the same level in the discourse structure) to provide descriptive information about that concept, these examples will appear after the descriptive explanation

Figure 8.9: Algorithm for determining the placement of examples in a description.

8.5.3 Effect of the Positioning on Other Factors

This section describes how the algorithm determines where the example can be presented, and its implications for other issues in the generation.[6] The cases that the system can encounter are:

- *the system finds an example to directly achieve the top-level discourse goal:* if the text type is intermediate,[7] the presentation of the example, followed by additional descriptive information elaborating on the features in the example satisfies the goal. In this case, the example is treated like a concept definition: the example is presented first, followed by an elaboration on the features in the example.

  Consider for instance, the description from (Winston and Horn, 1984) in figure 8.8. The description begins with an example followed by the explanation.[8] In such descriptions, the examples can be quite complex, depending upon the initial communicative goal.

- *the system finds an example that satisfies an intermediate level discourse goal:* if the text type is introductory, there are three possibilities for the system:

  1. the goal can be satisfied without using the example (only text is generated),

  2. the goal can be satisfied by presenting the example(s) (and some text may be elided), or

  3. the goal can be satisfied by presenting the example(s), as well as some text.

  The planner must now make a choice between these three possibilities, based on the context (the knowledge base, user model, as

---

[6]The effect of example positioning on the number of examples to be presented is discussed in the *Rhetoric* as well: "if they [examples] stand first, they resemble induction, and induction is not suitable to rhetorical speeches except in very few cases; if they stand last, they resemble evidence ... wherefore, it is necessary to quote a number of examples if they are put first, but one alone is sufficient if they are put last" (Aristotle, 1926) 2.20.1394a.

[7]The system reasons that in an intermediate text type, basic definitions of concepts are known to the intended user.

[8]While the description begins with a 'background' statement, this statement serves as background to the example, and in our system would be generated *as part of* the example.

well as the dialogue history). If either #2 or #3 are chosen, the
result will be examples interspersed within the description, as in
the description from (Touretzky, 1984) given in figure 8.8. The
choice is made as follows: if the definition of the concept has not
yet been presented, then the system cannot present examples at
that point, but must generate text (this is what happened in the
case of predicate-relation-form in section 7.3). If the definition has been presented, the goal is to elaborate upon a recursive,
or an anomalous feature (such as, for instance, a list of lists), then
the system generates both text and examples. Otherwise, the system presents only examples.

Consider the description from (Touretzky, 1984) in figure 8.8: the
first set of examples are used to illustrate two features about data
elements in a list: (a) the fact that the number of elements in
a list can vary, and (b) the type of elements in a list can also
vary. This fact could also have been expressed by a descriptive
explanation as in: *"The types of the elements of a list can be either atoms, numbers, or both"*, following the statement about the
number of elements. As can be seen in this description, the communicative goal of expressing the different types of elements is
satisfied by presenting a group of examples, causing the sentence
above (in italics) to be elided from the resulting description.

In the last example, when the system had a goal of elaborating
upon a list of lists, the system presented both the textual explanation, as well as an example.

- *the text type constraint prevents the generation of examples by
  communicative goals before the top-level goal to describe the concept has been achieved:* this is the case in reference texts as seen
  in the description from (Steele Jr., 1984) in figure 8.8. There are
  two important implications of postponing the presentation of examples until the complete description has been given:

  1. Since the text type constraints prevent the generation of ex-
     amples to satisfy intermediate level discourse goals immedi-
     ately, all intermediate level discourse goals *must be realized
     in text*. This implies that the textual description generated
     cannot have portions replaced by example elaboration, thus
     resulting in *descriptions that are comprehensive and com-
     plete*.

2. Since all the goals to generate examples are postponed till the end, examples that satisfy multiple goals can be generated. This results in examples that are more complex, have multiple features and illustrate more than one point. This results in the need to generate prompts with the examples to ensure that the user does not miss the points being made by the examples. Prompts may also become necessary because the examples may now be presented physically distant from the description.

We have presented our algorithm, and some of the implications that arise from the use of this algorithm in the generation of descriptions with examples. The algorithm has worked well in determining the placement of examples in descriptions generated by our system; in addition, the algorithm correctly predicted the position of examples in hand simulations of other texts in our corpus.

8.6　A Trace of the System

8.6.1　Text Type: Introductory

We now illustrate the working of the algorithm by describing the system as it plans the presentation of two descriptions of the LISP concept list in different text types. The two text types we consider are the introductory text and advanced text types. The descriptions of the concept list will be similar to the ones presented in figure 8.1 and 8.2. We have already described the generation of the description for an introductory text type in section 6.3. Therefore, we do not describe it again in detail, but present a high level view, and reiterate the places where the text type plays a role in the decision making process.

Given that the system needs to produce a description of a list for an introductory manual, the description is generated in a fashion identical to the one presented earlier: the system is given a top-level goal of (BEL HEARER (CONCEPT LIST)). The text planner searches for applicable plan operators in its plan-library, and selects one based on the applicable constraints. The text type restricts the choice of the features to present to be syntactic ones. The main features of list are retrieved, and two subgoals are posted: one to list the critical features (the left parenthesis, the data elements and the right parenthesis), and another to elaborate upon them.

The planner searches for appropriate operators to satisfy these goals. These goals result in the planner generating a plan for the first two sentences of figure 8.1.

The system needs to elaborate upon the data elements of a list. These can be of three types: numbers, symbols, or lists. The system can either communicate this information by realizing an appropriate sentence, or through examples — since it can generate examples for each of these types, or both. The introductory text type constraints cause the system to pick examples to satisfy this intermediate level discourse goal. If the text type had been advanced, the system would have delayed the presentation of examples, and text would have been generated at that point instead of the examples. The system posts two goals to illustrate the two dimensions along which the data elements can vary: the number of elements and the type.

At this point, the system can present a few complex, multi-featured examples of data-elements in a list, or it can present a larger number of simpler examples. The text type constraints force the system to choose the simple, single featured examples. Thus the planner generates a goal to present an example of each type: symbols, numbers, symbols and numbers, and sub-lists. Because the text type is introductory, the last data type, *sub-lists*, is marked by the planner as a *recursive* use of the concept, and has to be handled specially. In the case of an introductory text, such examples must be introduced with appropriate explanations added to the text. For this data type therefore, the planner realizes the goal through both text and examples. If the text type had been "advanced," the system would have generated a prompt denoting the presence of the sub-list. The resulting skeletal text-plan generated by the system is shown in Fig. 8.11. The resulting output is shown in the screen dump in figure 8.12.

8.6.2 Text Type: Advanced

Consider the second case, where the text type is specified as 'advanced.' The system starts with the same top-level goal as before, but the text type constraints cause the planner to select both the structural representation of a list, as well as the syntactic structure for presentation.

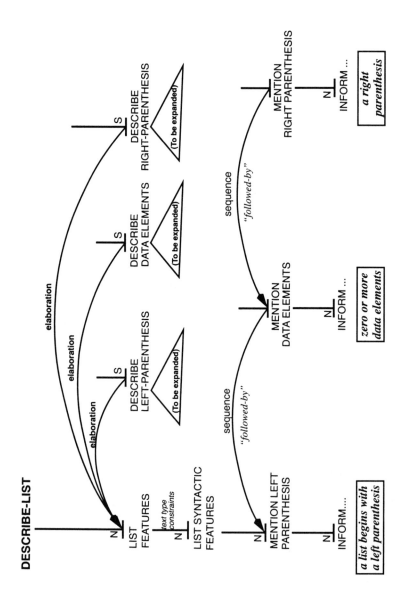

Figure 8.10: Skeletal plan for listing main features of list.

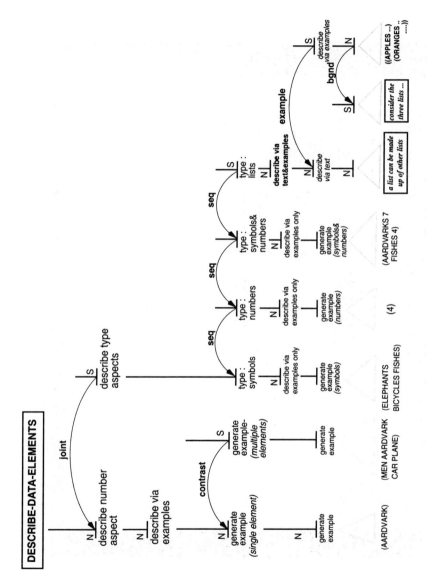

Figure 8.11: Skeletal plan for generating examples of lists.

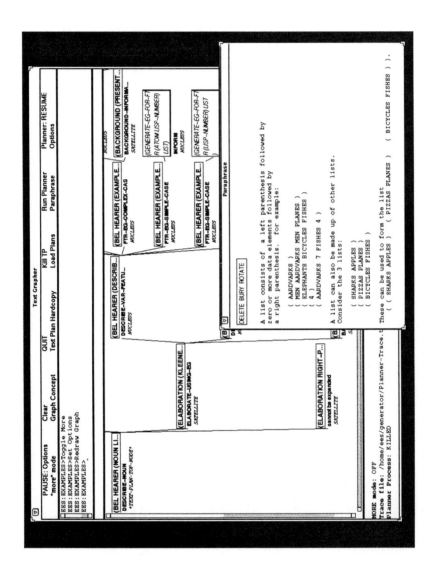

Figure 8.12: Generation of an introductory description of a `list`.

This results in the planner selecting the following features for presentation:[9]

Structural Features:
```
(ISA LIST
     (OR EMPTY-LIST
         (CONS-CELL  (CAR  :type  LIST-ELEMENTS
                           :name  "list-elements")
                     (CDR  :type  LIST
                           :name  "list"  )))))
```

Syntactic Features:
```
(LEFT-PARENTHESIS  (KLEENE-CLOSURE DATA-ELEMENTS)
                   RIGHT-PARENTHESIS
```

The planner posts two goals, one a NUCLEUS subgoal to describe the list textually, and a SATELLITE subgoal to present examples about it, related by the coherence relation EXAMPLE. (This results in the phrase "For example ... .") The NUCLEUS sub-goal is to describe a list (textually). It posts two NUCLEUS goals: one to describe the underlying structure, and one to describe the syntactic form of a list. These two goals are linked by the coherence relation JOINT (this is because, unlike SEQUENCE in the previous description, there is no particular ordering between the structural and syntactic descriptions here).

The goal to describe the structure paraphrases the feature as follows:

> A list is defined to be either the empty list or a CONS cell whose CDR component is a list. The CAR components of the CONSes are called elements of the list.

The planner queries the knowledge representation for any further information regarding a list. Two other facts are retrieved about the concept list-elements: there is a CONS cell for each element, and there are no elements in an empty-list. The planner generates English for these two facts as well. Both of these statements are linked to the (DESCRIBE (STRUCTURE LIST)) goal through the ELABORATE

---

[9]The structural element selected for paraphrasing is illustrated here in simplified fashion, rather than the LOOM notation for clarity.

coherence relation. The final output as a result of the (DESCRIBE (STRUCTURE LIST)) goal is:

> A list is defined to be either the empty list or a CONS cell whose CDR component is a list. The CAR components of the CONSes are called elements of the list. For each element of the list, there is a CONS cell. The empty list NIL has no elements.

The second sub-goal posted because of the top-level NUCLEUS goal is for generating a syntactic description of a list. Since the text type prevents the generation of any examples for intermediate level discourse goals, the sub-goal of (DESCRIBE (SYNTAX LIST)) results in a purely textual description. The generation of such a description is described in section 6.1, and will not be repeated here. Since our system does not currently address the phrasing issue, the description about the syntactic specification of a list is exactly the same as in the introductory case (without examples). The only difference is that since the text type is advanced, the system retrieves two additional types of data elements: characters and strings. These are not presented in introductory texts.[10] This results in the following output:

> A list consists of a left parenthesis, followed by zero or more data elements, followed by a right parenthesis. Data elements can be either symbols, numbers, characters, strings, lists, or a mixture thereof.

Because the advanced text type constrains the system from realizing any of the intermediate level discourse goals by presenting examples, the description generated so far is:

- free of any examples: the only examples presented are due to the top-level SATELLITE goal,

- the textual description is comprehensive: all the information is presented in the description, since examples cannot possibly cause the elision of text

---

[10]Both of these types are not defined in introductory texts before the list is described. Quite often, the character type is not mentioned through out the introductory book. We implemented our text type constraints to take these types to be 'advanced.'

The system still needs to expand the top level SATELLITE goal to present examples. This sub-goal is related to the NUCLEUS sub-goal through the EXAMPLE relation, which results in the generation of the "For example:" phrase between the two text spans which result from the nucleus and the satellite expansions. The text type constrains the system to generate as few examples as possible. Since at least two examples are required to show the variable nature of any feature, the system generates two examples of a list to illustrate the data elements. To generate the maximum contrast possible between two examples of a list, the system posts two goals: one each to generate examples of a list illustrating the following features:

Goal 1
generate example of list illustrating the fact that *data elements can be symbols*

Goal 2
generate example of list illustrating the fact that *data elements can be numbers, characters, lists, strings, or a mixture of all these*

In constructing the two examples, the system picks simple symbols for the first example, and complex instances to build the second example: thus the system selects a floating point number rather than an integer as an element of the list. The example generator also ensures that the lists generated are all of different lengths. The planner finds that the second example is recursive: there is a list as an element of the list. Since the planner cannot generate background text in this text type, the planner generates prompts for the examples.[11] The resulting text plan and output is shown in figures 8.13 and 8.14.

8.7 Discussion

We have presented an analysis of the differences in descriptions that integrate examples for introductory and advanced texts. The varia-

---

[11]The planner need only generate a prompt for the second example; however, in an attempt to replicate the texts in our corpus, the system generates prompts for all examples in a group if a prompt is necessary for one of them.

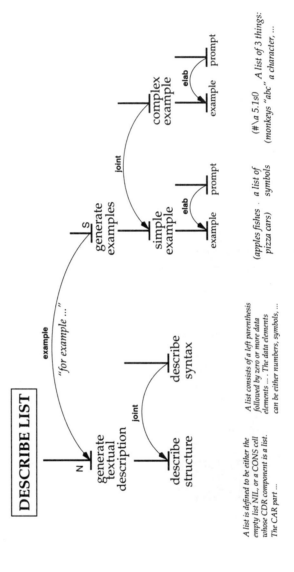

Figure 8.13: The generated text plan for one possible "reference manual" description of a list.

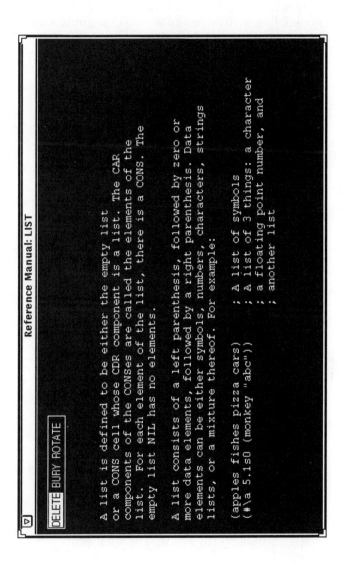

Figure 8.14: A snapshot of the system's description of the advanced description of a `list`.

tions occur not just in the descriptive part of the explanations, but also in the examples that accompany them. Since the examples and the descriptive component are tightly integrated and affect each other in many ways, a system designed to generate such descriptions must take into account these interactions and be able to structure the presentation accordingly. We have presented information necessary to generate descriptions for these two text types. The algorithm used by the system was illustrated by tracing the generation of two descriptions of the LISP list.

Chapter 9

Evaluation

The proof of the pudding is in the eating.
– Don Quixote de la Mancha[†]

The previous chapters have dealt with different aspects of the generation of descriptions with integrated examples. We enumerated the important issues involved, and presented system traces of the generation of various descriptions. However, the validity of the issues identified as relevant must be verified before acceptance. An empirical evaluation of the efficacy of the different issues involved can also help in gaining a better understanding of the relative importance of the issues. This chapter presents an evaluation of the different heuristics that the system uses.

[†]In (de Cervantes, 1981), p. 322.

9.1 Evaluating the Output

Evaluating Natural Language Generation (NLG) systems is a difficult task. A workshop on NLG evaluation (Hovy and Meteer, 1990) acknowledged the importance of evaluation, but did not reach any definite conclusion on how NLG systems may be evaluated. Previous approaches to this question have been based on an introspective analysis of the fluency of the generated text. Kukich (1983) and Mellish and Evans (1989) performed such an analysis for their systems. Although fluency is important, our emphasis in this case is to do with information presented in a useful and effective form. The descriptions generated by our system for the INTEND grammar were liked by the members of our project. The LISP descriptions were also considered very readable by participants who took part in our evaluation.

The main motivation for our system was the presentation of examples and their integration with the accompanying explanation. It is essential that the writer explicitly consider the communicative effects of each example on the reader and take these into account during the discourse planning process. This is important because examples and text strongly constrain each other, and explanations where these two components are not well integrated can cause a loss of comprehension (Chandler and Sweller, 1991), or even mislead the reader into making false implicatures or incorrect inferences from assumed information (Merrill and Tennyson, 1978). If the heuristics presented in this book allow the system to generate descriptions that minimize such occurrences, then the heuristics can be considered useful. To this end, we compared the presentations generated by using our heuristics to descriptions in text books to see the effect of a systematic application of our principles.

Appendix A presents seven descriptions of a `list` from popular introductory or texts on LISP. We analyzed each of these descriptions for their example presentations, and their integration with the textual explanation. Based on the requirements identified in various psychological studies, we consider that at least 5 of the descriptions do not satisfy all of the requirements in some form or the other, such as presenting examples ordered by complexity, or marking anomalous cases, etc. The remaining two descriptions do not violate these requirements, and are therefore good by these educational/cognitive standards. Given that the description generated by our system takes all of these factors into account, we consider our description to be of better than average quality, at least on the educational/cognitive scale.

The seven descriptions presented in appendix A illustrate some of the shortcomings that are often found in naturally occurring texts. This may be due to the fact that people are prone to write descriptions without keeping in mind all the different issues that can lead to reduced reader comprehension.[1] As an example of how some of these issues can be overlooked by people, consider for instance the examples presented in a description of a list in an advanced text (Steele Jr., 1984).

```
(a b c)                    ; a list of 3 symbols
(2.0s0 (a 1) #\*)          ; a list of 3 things: a floating point
                           ;   number, another list, and a
                           ;   character object
```

This description presents two lists (at the top level), both containing three elements. Given this description, the user may possibly generalize incorrectly that top-level lists must contain exactly three elements.

9.2   Evaluating the Issues

To test the validity and estimate the importance of the issues mentioned in section 3, we attempted to empirically evaluate the effect of each factor on the comprehensibility and ease of understanding descriptions containing examples. To do so, we generated two descriptions, one taking the factor into account, and the other specifically disregarding the factor.[2] Participants in the Study were then made to answer a set of questions, categorizing different examples as either belonging, or not belonging, to the concept under consideration.

The test participants were a number of graduate students in differ-

---

[1]After a discussion on these issues, a colleague once remarked to me that he had neglected to consider some of these issues in his writing; that explicitly taking these issues into consideration resulted in many changes to some of his presentations, and hopefully improving them.

[2]Some of these descriptions were generated by the system, by modifying the text planning operators to not consider specific issues; others were generated manually, specifically for the evaluation.

ent departments at the University of Southern California, Carnegie-
Mellon University and the University of Pittsburgh.[3] These participants may well represent the most likely initial users of such help facilities; all of them use advanced equipment almost constantly through-
out the day. All of these participants represented the naive user being
introduced to the domain. However, for more representative results,
these tests should ideally be administered on a broader cross section of
subjects with different backgrounds. An initial problem with the use of
graduate students was that they were very unwilling to be "beaten" by
a question; they would consequently spend large amounts of time reading and re-reading the description until they could answer the questions. The first few questionnaires were returned with almost all of the
answers marked correctly, although the time taken to answer the tests
differed drastically. We decided that the only way to test for relative
superiority among the concept descriptions was to limit the amount of
time available for answering the questions.[4] This forced the participants to try and understand the concept from the two descriptions in
similar amounts of time. The rest of the section describes the results
obtained in our study.

9.2.1   Descriptions With and Without Examples

There have been a number of studies on the usefulness of examples,
especially in documentation, for example, (Charney, Reder, and Wells,
1988), but we decided to see the results with our participants. These
were split into two groups. Four different concept descriptions were
given to the subjects. Each description had two versions: one with
examples, and another without examples which were given to the two
groups. One such pair of descriptions on the LISP function GENSYM is
shown in figure 9.1 and the questions are shown in figure 9.2.

The group given the description without the examples made between
4 and 11 mistakes out of the 21 questions. The average number of mistakes made were 6. (Most of these mistakes were around the notion
of the prefix being 'reset.') However, in the second group — the group
who were given the description with included examples — the maxi-

---

[3]Most of these tests were given to a groups containing 12–16 students. With the
exception of two students, the participants were not in Computer Science.

[4]This is the same approach taken in most of the standardized tests, such as the GRE,
SAT, etc.

```
(GENSYM &optional (PREFIX "G"))
```

GENSYM is a function call with an optional argument called PREFIX. It returns a new, uninterned symbol, whose print name begins with PREFIX and ends with a number; the number is incremented with each call to GENSYM and the default value of PREFIX is reset to whatever is passed as an argument to GENSYM.

```
(GENSYM &optional (PREFIX "G"))
```

GENSYM is a function call with an optional argument called PREFIX. For example:

```
(GENSYM)
(GENSYM "ABC")
```

The function returns a new, uninterned symbol, whose print name begins with PREFIX and ends with a number. For example:

```
(GENSYM "ABC")   ==> #:ABC26
```

The number is incremented with each call to GENSYM.

```
(GENSYM "ABC")   ==> #:ABC27
(GENSYM "ABC")   ==> #:ABC28
```

The default value of PREFIX is reset to whatever string is passed as an argument to GENSYM.

```
(GENSYM "USC")   ==> #:USC29
(GENSYM)         ==> #:USC30
```

Figure 9.1: Descriptions with and without examples.

FUNCTION CALL	OUTPUT	CORRECT	INCORRECT
(GENSYM)	⟹	**ERROR!**	☐	☐
(GENSYM)	⟹	#:G27	☐	☐
(GENSYM "ABC")	⟹	#:ABC27	☐	☐
(GENSYM "ABC")	⟹	#:GABC27	☐	☐
(GENSYM "ABC")	⟹	#:GABC27#:GABC28		☐
(GENSYM "ABC")	⟹	#:ABC28	☐	☐
(GENSYM)	⟹	#:G29	☐	☐
(GENSYM)	⟹	#:G30	☐	☐
(GENSYM)	⟹	#:ABC31	☐	☐
(GENSYM)	⟹	#:ABC29	☐	☐
(GENSYM)	⟹	#:ABC30	☐	☐
(GENSYM "ABC")	⟹	#:ABC30ABC31	☐	☐
(GENSYM "G")	⟹	#:ABC30G32	☐	☐
(GENSYM)	⟹	#:G27	☐	☐
(GENSYM)	⟹	#:G28	☐	☐
(GENSYM "#:G28")	⟹	#:G2829	☐	☐
(GENSYM)	⟹	#:G32	☐	☐
(GENSYM "XYZ")	⟹	#:XYZ27	☐	☐
(GENSYM "XYZ")	⟹	#:XYZ#:XYZ27	☐	☐
(GENSYM "XYZ")	⟹	#:XYZ#:XYZ#:XYZ27	☐	☐

Figure 9.2: Questionnaire on GENSYM used to test effectiveness of examples.

mum number of mistakes made by people was 4 (the average number of mistakes was 2), and there were 6 people who made no mistakes. The results indicate that the inclusion of examples helped clarify the issues for the users.

9.2.2 Positioning the Example

It is important that examples be placed appropriately with respect to the accompanying text. We have seen in previous chapters how examples can sometimes occur before the text, within the text, and after the text, depending upon the text type. Empirical studies have shown that in the case of introductory users, the best placement of examples seems to be *immediately following* the point they are supposed to illustrate. We presented the descriptions shown in figure 9.3 and 9.4 to our test participants, who were novices with respect to TeX. For a description with examples *before* the explanation, we used the same description as in figure 9.3, with the positions of the example and the explanation interchanged.

The test participants were split into three groups, one for each description. Each of the groups was given a minute to study the descriptions (this is the time it takes to read the description twice). The participants were made to answer 10 questions related to the stacking operator in TeX. In the group with interspersed examples, only one person made a mistake. In the group with examples after the description, 5 participants made an average of 3 mistakes, as compared to 6 participants making an average of 3 mistakes for the group with the examples before the description.

In the case of naive users therefore, the placement of examples immediately after the concept's definition seems the most beneficial.

9.2.3 Presentation of Different Example Types

Chapter 4 dealt with the different example types in our system. According to our categorization, examples can vary along three dimensions: their polarity with respect to the definition they accompany, the text type for which they are generated, and the knowledge type of which they happen to be instances. For a concept therefore, an example (and

Stacking operations are used in TeX to produce fractions: \over produces fractions with the argument on the left hand side becoming the numerator, and the right hand side argument becoming the denominator. Other variations of \over are:

- \atop which leaves out the fraction bar
- \above which provides a fraction bar of a specified thickness
- \choose which leaves out the fraction bar and encloses the construct in parentheses
- \brace which leaves out the fraction bar and encloses the construct in braces
- \brack which leaves out the fraction bar and encloses the construct in brackets.

For example:

```
$${n+1 \over n-1}         \qquad {n+1 \atop n-1}    \qquad
  {n+1 \above 2pt n-1} \qquad {n+1 \choose n-1} \qquad
  {n+1 \brace n-1}         \qquad {n+1 \brack n-1}$$
```

produces:

$$\frac{n+1}{n-1} \qquad \begin{matrix} n+1 \\ n-1 \end{matrix} \qquad \frac{n+1}{n-1} \qquad \binom{n+1}{n-1} \qquad \left\{ \begin{matrix} n+1 \\ n-1 \end{matrix} \right\} \qquad \left[\begin{matrix} n+1 \\ n-1 \end{matrix} \right]$$

Figure 9.3: Description with examples after the description.

\over produces fractions, with the argument on the left hand side becoming the numerator, and the right hand side argument becoming the denominator. For instance: $\${n+1 \backslash over\ n-1}\$$ produces

$$\frac{n+1}{n-1}$$

Other variations of \over are: \atop which leaves out the fraction bar. For instance: $\${n+1 \backslash atop\ n-1}\$$ produces:

$$n+1$$
$$n-1$$

\above which provides a fraction bar of a specified thickness. Thus: $\${n+1 \backslash above\ 2pt\ n-1}\$$ produces:

$$n+1$$
$$\rule{2cm}{1.5pt}$$
$$n-1$$

\choose which leaves out the fraction bar and encloses the construct in parentheses, as in: $\${n+1 \backslash choose\ n-1}\$$ which produces:

$$\binom{n+1}{n-1}$$

\brace which leaves out the fraction bar and encloses the construct in braces, as in: $\${n+1 \backslash brace\ n-1}\$$, which produces:

$$\begin{Bmatrix} n+1 \\ n-1 \end{Bmatrix}$$

and \brack which leaves out the fraction bar and encloses the construct in brackets, as in $\${n+1 \backslash brack\ n-1}\$$, which produces

$$\begin{bmatrix} n+1 \\ n-1 \end{bmatrix}$$

Figure 9.4: Description with examples within the description.

its associated presentation) can be varied along the polarity and the text type. In this section, we consider the issue of polarity.

The polarity of an example can either be positive, negative, or anomalous. The importance of negative examples in concept learning has already been shown by empirical studies (Feldman, 1972; Houtz, Moore, and Davis, 1973). However, we are not aware of studies on the presentation of anomalous examples with, or apart (marked as specifically different) from the regular examples.[5] Therefore, we decided to study the differences in the presentation of anomalous examples together with, and apart from the normal examples.

Consider the two descriptions of the UNIX command **who** shown in figures 9.5 and 9.6. In the case of figure 9.5, even though the description talks only about files as being arguments to the command, the examples presented include the two[6] anomalous cases of **who**. The distinction between the normal arguments to **who** (files) and the exceptional cases of **who** are much more clearly marked in figure 9.6. This is clearly a case of an anomalous example, since by the classification presented in chapter 4, anomalous examples are defined to include instances that are examples, but are not covered by the definition. In the evaluation, all of the participants given the first description (with unmarked anomalous examples) got all questions of the form:

```
who is <user-name>
who <user-name>
```

wrong.[7] Only 2 out of the 6 people given the second description with marked analogous examples got questions of this type wrong. It would seem therefore that it is important to separate and explicitly present anomalous examples as such.

9.2.4 Complexity and Number of Examples

As we have already stated in chapter 3, the more the number of features illustrated in each example, the less the number of examples re-

---

[5]Though this has been suggested in (Engelmann and Carnine, 1982).

[6]The command *whoami* is not considered here, since by UNIX standards, it is not a special form of the *who am i* command, but an entirely different one.

[7]People with some previous exposure to UNIX were especially prone to making errors in the first case because of the presence of the whois command in UNIX.

---

who: When used without arguments, **who** lists the login
name, terminal name, and login time for each current user.
When a file name is specified, **who** examines its contents
and lists it as shown:

```
example% who
   ramesh    console Aug 23 09:34
   ramesh    ttyp0   Aug 24 14:19   (:0.0)
   macgreg   ttyp2   Sep  2 09:36   (128.9.208.151:0.)
   mittal    ttypb   Sep  4 11:18   (seuss.isi.edu)

example% who /var/adm/wtmp
   mittal    ttyp5   Feb 12 13:13 (power-chow.isi.e)
   mittal    ttyp5   Feb 12 13:15 (power-chow.isi.e)
   ees       ttyp7   Feb 12 13:24 (doc.isi.edu)
   koda      ttyp7   Feb 12 13:30 (rising.isi.edu)

example% who am i
   doc.isi.edu!mittal ttypb Sep 4 11:18 (seuss.isi.edu)

example% who is who
   doc.isi.edu!mittal ttypb Sep 4 11:18 (seuss.isi.edu)
```

Figure 9.5: Description with anomalous examples not explicitly
marked.

---

who: When used without arguments, **who** lists the login
name, terminal name, and login ... [lines deleted] ... contents. Examples of the usage of **who** are:

```
example% who
   ramesh   console Aug 23 09:34
   ⋮
   koda   ttyp7 Feb 12 13:30 (rising.isi.edu)
```

However, there are two cases in which the argument to **who**
need not be a file name. **who** can be used to find out who
you are logged in as: it displays your hostname, login name,
terminal name, and login time.

```
example% who am i
   doc.isi.edu!mittal ttypb Sep 4 11:18 (seuss.isi.edu)

example% who is who
   doc.isi.edu!mittal ttypb Sep 4 11:18 (seuss.isi.edu)
```

Figure 9.6: Description with anomalous examples clearly marked.

quired to illustrate all the features of the concept. Even if the same number of examples are used in two cases, one with simple examples, and one with complex multi-featured examples, the descriptions are likely to be understood to different extents. In our test, we asked our volunteers to look at two descriptions that featured the FORMAT statement in LISP and then answer questions on simple aspects of the FORMAT statement.[8] The description with the two sets of examples is shown in figure 9.7.

We conducted two tests with these descriptions: in the first case, four members of the group were given the description and the three simple examples. The second group was given the description with the three complex examples, while the third group was given the description with only the last example. The first group got all their answers right, while the second group made an average of 2 mistakes out of the 10 questions (one person got all the answers correct). The third group, which was given a single question, fared the worst, with none of the four getting all the answers correct, and the average number of mistakes per person being 3.25.

In another test on the number of examples required, the participants were given more examples than the number of features being illustrated. The success rate did not rise significantly beyond that in which the each example illustrated one feature. It would thus appear that the larger the number of examples presented to naive users, the better their understanding of the concept.

9.2.5 Presentation Order of Examples

It is important that the examples be presented in the correct sequence. Since examples are not generated in isolation, but with associated material such as prompts, background information, or contrasting negative examples, the associated information will also be moved around if the example moves away from its correct position in the sequence. An instance of this can be seen in figure 9.2.5, where the original description of a list (described in section 6.3) was generated with the ordering constraint on the plan operators reversed. The system generated the goals to elaborate upon the data elements of a list. To satisfy

---

[8]The last example shown in figure 9.7 was accompanied with extra information that gave the values for '(get-name person)', and so on.

FORMAT is a powerful, generalized string manipulation function. FOR-
MAT takes three types of arguments: a stream on which to write (this
can be NIL), a control string containing directives, and the information
to be used by the directives. Different directives are used to process
different types of data to be inserted into the output string. a is used
for ASCII strings, while c is used to print characters, and d to print
integers in decimal notation.

Simple Examples:

```
(format nil "Blue Bird") ⟹ "Blue Bird"

(format nil "~a" "Green Grass") ⟹ "Green Grass"

(format nil "Its a ~A! Its a ~A!" "bird" "plane")
    ⟹ "Its a bird! Its a plane!"

(format nil "~a~%~a" "who?" "what?") ⟹
    "who?
     what?"
```

Complex Examples:

```
(format nil "The answer is ~ D." (expt 47 5)) ⟹
    "The answer is 229,345,007."

(format nil "Type ~C to ~A."
            (set-char-bit #\D :control t)
            "delete all files")
    ⟹ "Type Control-D to delete all files."

(format nil "~% Name: ~a~% ~a~a" (get-name person)
    (if (get-address person) (get-address person)
        "No known address")
    (if (get-age person)
        (format nil "~a:~a" "Age:" (get-age person)))))
```

Figure 9.7: Descriptions with simple and complex examples.

A list begins with a left parenthesis. Then come zero or more pieces of data (called the elements of a list) and a right parenthesis. A list may contain other lists as elements. Given the three lists:

```
(BLUE SKY)  (GREEN GRASS)  (BROWN EARTH)
```

we can make a list by combining them all with a parentheses

```
((BLUE SKY)  (GREEN GRASS)  (BROWN EARTH))
```

Other examples are:

```
(3 FRENCH FRIES)
(RED ORANGE GRAPE CAR)
(RED YELLOW GREEN BLUE)
(AARDVARK)
(2 3 5 11 19)
```

Figure 9.8: One possible description of list, with no ordering imposed on the presentation of the examples.

this goal, the system needed to present examples of lists in which the data-elements were atoms, numbers, lists, and a mixture of the above. The system chose (because of reversed ordering) to satisfy the goal of presenting a list of lists first. However, since this is a recursive case, the system was forced to present background material in the form of other lists, resulting the description presented in figure 9.2.5, which does not resemble any of the descriptions we have observed in our corpus. This figure also illustrates again the strong mutual interaction of the examples and text in a description. Changing any of the factors that affect one is likely to affect the other as well. From this description, it is clear that ordering is an important factor in ensuring the overall description generated is coherent and useful. In other descriptions, where the description took into account the pairing of positive and negative examples for critical features and the pairs were ordered by the complexity of the feature being illustrated, the group that was given the ordered description fared better (2 mistakes out of 10) than the group which did not (6 mistakes on the average).

9.2.6   Need for Prompts

Figure 9.9: Output generated by code in figure 9.10.

As we have mentioned previously (section 3.8), prompts are usually seen in reference texts, where complex examples illustrating multiple points are presented. Prompts serve to highlight factors in the example that may not have been mentioned immediately before the example is presented. To test for the efficacy of prompts in the presence of such descriptions, we presented our participants with relatively long descriptions (more than 10 lines) from different books and presented multi-featured examples, with and without prompts to them. An instance of the multi-featured example presented in this evaluation is shown in figure 9.10. The same example was used, once with prompts as shown, and once without prompts. (The postscript code generates the output shown in figure 9.9). The description accompanying these examples in the test was a page from (McGilton and Campione, 1992). The group given the example with prompts fared better than the one without prompts: the average number of mistakes made in the two groups were 3 and 5, out of a possible 12 questions. Thus, it would seem that prompts play a useful role in certain text types.

9.3 Discussion

The evaluation reported in this chapter on the effect of different factors in the generation of integrated descriptions indicate their importance and necessity for coherence and comprehensibility. This chapter presented some of the descriptions that were used in the evaluation. There are undoutedly many ways in which the evaluation could have been improved: for instance, the number of participants could have been increased, the issues could have been analyzed at finer levels of detail, and statistical correlations derived. However, due to a lack of both resources and time, we conducted the limited experiments described here. These experiments suggest that the issues identified from the corpus analysis may be worth further study. This skeletal evaluation served that goal satisfactorily: each of the issues tested for did indeed suggest a correlation with comprehension. Thus, it may be useful to further consider these, and related issues, in the design of systems meant to generate descriptions integrating text and examples together.

An important issue that we discussed briefly in section 9.1 was on how closely the descriptions generated by our system matched those found in naturally occurring texts. It is important to state here that our system cannot generate any descriptions that depend upon the underlying semantics in any way because we do not have represent these semantics now. Almost all of the texts in our corpus show some variation in their writing style, even among the reference manuals. In most cases, this is because while the major part of the manual may have been written by one person (albeit over a long period of time), there are

```
%!PS
/inch { 72 mul } def          % define inch procedure
306 396 270 0 360 arc         % draw a circle
closepath                     % finish circle
gsave                         % remember graphics state
    0.50 setgray              % medium gray shade
    fill                      % fill circle
grestore                      % restore graphics state
72 setlinewidth               % fat line width
stroke                        % paint outline of circle
/Palatino-Bold findfont       % find a font
360 scalefont                 % make letters large
setfont                       % set current font
96 275 moveto                 % position current point
(PS) false charpath           % get character path
gsave                         % remember graphics state
    18 setlinewidth           % fat line width
    stroke                    % paint outline of characters
grestore                      % restore graphics state
1.0 setgray                   % white color
fill                          % fill character outlines
showpage                      % display page
```

Figure 9.10: Example used in testing the effect of prompts.

often sections that are written by other authors. Thus, for instance, in the case of the LISP manual (Steele Jr., 1984), whole chapters (on format and loop, for instance) have been written by other people. Writing styles can thus vary even within the same book. An example of such a book is the one on LISP programming by Winston and Horn (1984); on the other hand, some of the manuals, or reference texts in our corpus, were written in a very rigid format, for instance, the early Lisp manuals (Meehan, 1979; McCarthy et al., 1985).

Our heuristics cover approximately 80% of the texts that we have seen in our corpus. The figure refers to how often our heuristics matched naturally occurring texts in the following criteria: (a) the position of the examples with respect to the explanation; (b) if the example(s) are within the explanation, the point at which the example(s) occur; (c) type of examples (i.e., single featured, positive, negative, etc); (d) the order of presentation of the examples; (e) the communication of information through text, examples, and both; (f) the presence or absence of anomalous examples and their treatment; (g) the presence of background explanation and examples for recursive cases, and (h) the use of prompts. The figure does not take into account the actual examples themselves, i.e., whether the quality of the examples generated by the example generator component matched the quality of examples found in our corpus. This was due to the use of only syntactic and type knowledge by our system in the example generation process. Since the current implementation does not represent, or reason with, the semantics of the different constructs, the actual examples generated are often quite unlike the ones seen in the corpus. Examples in naturally occurring texts are usually written by taking into account the semantics of the construct, their typical usage, and the non-syntactic relationships between different parts of the examples. This will be seen clearly in appendix D, where some of the descriptions planned by the system are presented.

Chapter 10

Conclusions

Everybody talks about documentation,
but nobody does anything about it.

— Anonymous

This document has argued for the presentation of examples in user help and automatically generated documentation. Documentation is an important factor in user acceptance of any system; it is essential that a system designed to automatically generate documentation be able to generate descriptions that include examples. Previous approaches to the generation of descriptions did not address the issue of presenting examples as an integrated part of a coherent description. This book has presented one approach to the planning and presentation of such descriptions that integrate examples and text.

10.1 Insights

There are a number of issues that must be identified and addressed if a system is to be designed to plan complex descriptions that involve both text and examples. In this work, we presented these issues — based on a synthesis of results in related fields such as educational psychology, as well as our own corpus analysis — and showed how they may be addressed in a computational framework to succesfully plan the presentation of complex descriptions that include examples. Some of the insights gained from this work are:

- the synthesis of results and ideas from different fields on the generation and presentation of good examples for learning and understanding;

- the identification and analysis of the different ways that examples and text influence each other (deletion and addition of text under specific circumstances);

- the specification of the different factors that are important in the context of natural language generation (i.e., the position of the examples, the type of examples, prompts, etc.);

- a new and improved categorization of example types that takes into account the context of the examples;

- the finding that interesting negative examples are not only useful, but can affect the choice of the positive examples;

- the identification of the differences between descriptions (in the BNF-documentation domain) generated for introductory texts and advanced texts;

- a validation of these claims by implementation of a system to generate such descriptions;

- an empirical evaluation of the cognitive effectiveness of some of the heuristics developed in the course of this research.

10.2   Limitations of the Work

There are some issues that we did not address in this work. One of these was the generation of descriptions for intermediate texts (intended for users between the introductory, naive users and the advanced, expert users): such descriptions (and the associated examples) are very 'use' oriented, that is, they illustrate different ways in which the concept could be made use of. For instance, in the case of a list, the typical descriptions seen are about how lists can be used to associate names and phone numbers, write functions, etc. For the system to be able to generate descriptions of this sort, the representation of the concept would have to include its typical uses, along with examples of each use.

Perhaps the greatest limitation of this work was this lack of a semantic representation for the constructs. This lack of semantic representation prevented us from generating not only intermediate texts, but also from generating meaningful descriptions of constructs such as loop and let forms. Such a representation was not explored here; we looked at the generation of descriptions and examples of only the syntactic form from an underlying representation that was generated almost automatically from the BNF representation. The issue of representing the semantics is, however, a problem of knowledge representation; given the appropriate knowledge of the semantics, the system would be able to take the knowledge into account and generate suitable descriptions.[1]

Some of the problems this caused our system can be seen in the descriptions for the let-form shown in figure 10.1. The fact that the BNF form does not specify that the variables declared initially in the let-form are usually then used in the body of the let-form causes the system to generate examples of let-forms that reflect this lack of knowledge. The last example also shows how this lack of semantic representation can cause the system to generate a syntactically correct, but semantically incorrect example where the unbound variable "apples" is assigned its own undefined value. Such problems are compounded in the case of a the description for a function-form (described in appendix D), where the parameters, the keyword arguments, and the optional arguments have different implications on their presence or absence which is not recognized in the BNF specification. To a lesser extent, the same problem affects the system in generating examples of a list: examples of lists in our corpus were of the form (BLUE SKY), (GREEN GRASS), or (3 FRENCH FRIES). Since there is no representation of the relationship between each of the elements, the examples

---

[1]One of the goals of EES was to design a knowledge representation scheme for precisely this reason: explainability. It has a sophisticated and complex representation for actions, operators, their effects, etc. In the current implementation, we have attempted to generate descriptions at the purely syntactic level to see how useful such descriptions may be without extensively representing each construct in the system.

The let-form consists of a left parenthesis followed by the word LET followed by a list of local variables followed by a number of forms. Finally, there is a right parenthesis. A local variable is specified as a list of the variable name which is a symbol and an initial value. Examples of let-forms are:

```
(LET ((ORANGES FISHES))
     MEN)
(LET ((BICYCLES 3) (PIZZAS 'MEN))
     2 9 CARS)
(LET ((YELLOW SKY) (FISHES BLUE))
     (MEN AARDVARKS))
(LET ((APPLES APPLES) (FISHES SHARKS))
     ((MEN CARS) (MEN BLUE)))
```

Figure 10.1: Explanation of a let-form planned by the system.

generated by the system do not emulate these naturally occuring examples.

These shortcomings on the part of the current implementation can be overcome if the semantics of the constructs and the relationship between the different parts of these constructs are represented in the system. The semantics would need to be represented using a language that both the text planner and the example generator would be able to understand and reason with during the planning process. Such a representation could also be augmented with stereotypical uses of the constructs; this would allow the system to generate intermediate texts with examples.

Another aspect that we did not address in depth in this work was the issue of generating descriptions of relations and processes; only concept descriptions were considered here. There are many similarities and some differences between descriptions generated about concepts and descriptions about relations and processes. Many of the issues raised earlier, such as determining the number of examples, determining critical and variable features, sequencing based on example complexity, integration with the textual description, and so on, remain the same. However, the *examples* themselves generated for relations and processes are different from those of concepts. For instance, in the case of relations, the examples are not of the relation itself, but consist of n-tuples of instances, where n is the arity of the relation, and the instances are objects between which the relation holds. Thus, to generate such examples, the system must first generate examples for the different concepts that the relation exists between; such examples (for each concept) would need to follow all of the issues presented in this book, such as that of complexity, sequencing, prompts, etc. Each example for the relation would then need to be evaluated in terms of complexity, critical features, etc. in terms of the relation definition, as well as the examples of the different constituent concepts. Similarly, *process-examples* are also quite different from *concept-examples* and *relation-examples*, because each process-example can require the presentation of a number of relation-examples, thus compounding the issues that need be considered.

Our research did not address any issues relating to the lexical choice or phrasing in this work. We also did not touch upon the issues of either formatting or the presentation of graphical examples (pictures or diagrams). Each of these issues is a very complicated one, and is currently not considered by the system.

Perhaps one of the most important limitations of this work was the application domain used: programming languages. Although all of the issues described in chapter 3 on the integration of examples with text remain valid in other domains as well, the heuristics on determining the relative complexity of an element and finding interesting negative examples will no longer be applicable. Also, the the differences between introductory and advanced texts will almost certainly be different in other domains.

10.3 Possible Extensions

There are a number of exciting directions where this work can be extended. These include:

- *Multi-media Generation:* Consider, for instance, an application such as automated multi-media generation, as in the COMET system (Elhadad et al., 1991; Feiner and McKeown, 1991), the WIP system (Wahlster et al., 1991; Wahlster et al., 1993), or the SAGE system (Roth, Mattis, and Mesnard, 1991; Roth and Hefley, 1993): in these cases, the system must necessarily reason about the communicative effects (both intended effects as well as implicatures) of the text and the alternative media (in the case of each of the three systems mentioned here, the parallel medium was graphics/images). In these cases, the issues that come to fore are very similar to those that had to be addressed in this work: how many images should be displayed, how complex should each image be, what should the position of the image be (before, within, or after the text), whether prompts should be used within the image (arrows, text, or other rhetorical devices, such as blinking, pulsing and animation). Thus, in both cases, the effect on the explanation must be explicitly considered by the system *during* the discourse planning process. Other similarities abound: for instance, specific features can be highlighted by presenting two identical pictures, with the feature to be highlighted being the only difference. Much of the reasoning (sequence of pictures, order of presentation, and so on) in multi-media generation and example presentation is very similar in nature.

  Although it is clear that the solutions we devised for examples in the BNF domain will not work for any arbitrary choice of a parallel medium, especially a more complex medium such as pictures, it is to be hoped that many of the issues raised in simpler, better understood domains containing only textual rhetorical devices might partially transfer over to models for multi-media generation. In fact, BNF being a generic, domain- and task-neutral specification formalism, has previously been used to represent a wide variety of domains and tasks such as mechanical device design (Mohd-Hashim, Juster, and de Pennington, 1994), protein-structure mapping (George, Mewes, and Kihara, 1987) and interface requirements (Reisner, 1981). The approach described here should transfer relatively straightforwardly, with some caveats, to any of these domains represented in BNF.

- *Critiquing Systems:* There are many similarities between explanation generation and critiquing: they both involve explaining aspects of the system to the user in natural language. However, there are also many differences between an explanation and a critique. For instance, while an explanation can be blunt and to the point, a critique must be phrased very differently, so that it plays up the positive aspects of the user's solution, and tactfully suggests better alternatives for the incorrect aspects of the solution.

Presenting counter examples for the weak points (or gaps) in the solution could help convince the user more effectively than a plain statement. The WEST system, with its pre-enumerated examples, was very successful in its critic's role in mathematics. The example generator would need to generate good counter-examples.

- *Knowledge Acquisition*: An interesting extension of such a system would be in the application area of knowledge acquisition. Should the system's internal representation be faulty or incomplete, the explanations generated by the system will also be faulty or incomplete. Such gaps and inconsistencies are more easily noticeable in the form of a wrong example than in a text. Given that the discourse structure represents the relationship of the example to the text and the internal representation, it is possible for the system to modify the knowledge representation based on the user's input about a faulty example. There are at least three advantages of using explanations with examples over plain text explanations in knowledge acquisition: (a) given that there are multiple examples are presented for each feature, an indication of a faulty example can be much more precise (and helpful to the system) than finding that a fault with the feature in general; (b) no additional parsing capability on the part of the system is required, beyond a means of indicating a faulty example; (c) should the system desire further elaborations, it can generate other, single-featured examples for clarification. Appendix C discusses some of these aspects in the context of some experiments that were conducted after the main body of this work was completed..

- *Presenting Analogies and Examples*: There are many similarities in the presentation of analogies and examples in natural language explanations. The discourse structure can be used in both cases to partition the set of features to try and find suitable analogies for presentation.[2] Analogies are more open-ended than ex-

---

[2] An initial attempt to make use of analogies in explanation using this framework can be seen in (Mittal and Paris, 1992).

amples, and there are many other issues that will need to be considered if they are to be incorporated. However, the framework would remain essentially the same.

In general, planning a presentation requires that the effects and implicatures regarding all aspects of the presentation be modelled, either explicitly or implicitly, by the planning process. This body of work shows how even "simple" extensions, such as examples, to purely expository text can result in the need to understand the extensions and their effects thoroughly and design appropriate planning strategies. Furthermore, because the presence of such extensions can also affect the surrounding context, the initial set of discourse strategies must also be modified. This book has described the issues that arise in one such case; as discussed above (and in Appendix C), there are a number of applications to which this work can be easily extended.

Bibliography

Abrahams, Paul W., Karl Berry, and Kathryn A. Hargreaves. 1990. *TEX for the Impatient*. Addison-Wesley Publishing Co.

Aleven, Vincent and Kevin D. Ashley. 1992. Automated Generation of Examples for a Tutorial in Case-Based Argumentation. In *Proceedings of the Second International Conference on Intelligent Tutoring Systems (ITS-92)*, Montreal, Canada.

Anderson, J. R. and M. Matessa. 1990. A Rational Analysis of Categorization. In Bruce W. Porter and Raymond J. Mooney, editors, *Proceedings of the Seventh International Conference on Machine Learning*, Austin, TX.

Anderson, John R. 1987. Skill acquisition: Compilation of weak-method problem solutions. *Psychological Review*, 94:192–210.

Anderson, John R., P. J. Kline, and C. M. Beasley. 1980. Complex Learning Processes. In R. E. Snow, P. A. Frederico, and W. E. Montague, editors, *Aptitude, Learning and Instruction*. Lawrence Erlbaum Associates, Hillsdale, NJ.

Angluin, Dana. 1987. Queries and Concept Learning. *Machine Learning*, 2(4):319–342.

Aristotle. 1926. *The "Art" of Rhetoric*. Loeb Classical Library. Edited and translated by John Henry Freese.

Aristotle. 1967. *Poetics*. University of Michgan Press, Ann Arbor, MI. Edited and translated by Gerald F. Else.

Ashley, Kevin and Vincent Aleven. 1992. Generating dialectical examples automatically. In *Proceedings of the Tenth National Conference on Artificial Intelligence (AAAI-92)*, pages 654–660, San Jose, CA. American Association for Artificial Intelligence.

Ashley, Kevin D. 1991. Reasoning with cases and hypotheticals in HYPO. *International Journal of Man-Machine Studies*, 34(6):753–796, June.

Bateman, John A. and Cécile L. Paris. 1989. Phrasing a Text in Terms the User can Understand. In *Proceedings of the 11th International Joint Conference on Artificial Intelligence*, pages 568–576, Detroit, MI, August.

Baxter, Rohan. 1989. SETTER: An Algebraic Problem Generator. Honors Thesis, Department of Computer Science, Monash University, Australia, October.

Beard, Richard E. and Peter V. Calamars. 1983. A Method for Designing Computer Support Documentation. Master's thesis, Department of Communication, AFIT/LSH, WPAFB, OH 45433, September.

Bell, Paula and Charlotte Evans. 1989. *Mastering Documentation*. John Wiley and Sons, Inc.

Biber, Douglas. 1988. *Variation across speech and writing*. Cambridge University Press, Cambridge, England.

Biber, Douglas. 1989. A typology of English Texts. *Linguistics*, 27:3–43.

Borde, Arvind. 1992. *TEX by Example*. Academic Press, Boston.

Braswell, Frank Merritt. 1989. *Inside Postscript*. Peachpit Press, Mobile, AL.

Brockmann, R. John. 1986. *Writing Better Computer User Documentation: From Paper to Online*. John Wiley and Sons, New York.

Brockmann, R. John. 1990. *Writing Better Computer User Documentation: From Paper to Hypertext*. John Wiley and Sons, New York.

Bruner, Jerome S. 1966. *Toward a Theory of Instruction*. Oxford University Press, London, U.K.

Burton, Richard R. and John Seely Brown. 1982. An Investigation of Computer Coaching for Informal Learning Activities. In Derek Sleeman and John Seely Brown, editors, *Intelligent Tutoring Systems*. Academic Press, Inc., chapter 4, pages 79–98.

Carnine, Douglas W. 1980a. Three Procedures for Presenting Minimally Different Positive and Negative Instances. *Journal of Educational Psychology*, 72(4):452–456.

Carnine, Douglas W. 1980b. Two Letter Discrimination Sequences: High-Confusion-Alternatives First versus Low-Confusion-Alternatives First. *Journal of Reading Behaviour*, XII(1):41–47, Spring.

Carnine, Douglas W. and Wesley C. Becker. 1982. Theory of Instruction: Generalisation Issues. *Educational Psychology*, 2(3–4):249–262.

Chandler, Paul and John Sweller. 1991. Cognitive Load Theory and the Format of Instruction. *Cognition and Instruction*, 8(4):292–332.

Charney, Davida H., Lynne M. Reder, and Gail W. Wells. 1988. Studies of Elaboration in Instructional Texts. In Stephen Doheny-Farina, editor, *Effective Documentation: What we have learned from Research*. The MIT Press, Cambridge, MA., chapter 3, pages 48–72.

Charniak, Eugene, Christopher K. Riesbeck, Drew V. McDermott, and James R. Meehan. 1987. *Artificial Intelligence Programming*. Lawrence Erlbaum Associates, Hillsdale, NJ.

Chi, Michelene T. H., Miriam Bassok, Matthew W. Lewis, Peter Reimann, and Robert Glaser. 1989. Self-Explanations: How Students Study and Use Examples in Learning to Solve Problems. *Cognitive Science*, 13(2):145–182, April-June.

Chinell, David F. 1990. *System Documentation: The In-Line Approach*. John Wiley and Sons, Inc.

Clark, D. C. 1971. Teaching Concepts in the Classroom: A Set of Prescriptions derived from Experimental Research. *Journal of Educational Psychology Monograph*, 62:253–278.

Cook, Diane J. 1989. ANAGRAM: An Analogical Planning System. Technical Report UIUCDCS-R-89-1561, Department of Computer Science, University of Illinois, Urbana-Champaign, December.

Cooper, Doug and Michael Clancey. 1982. *Oh! Pascal!* W. W. Norton and Co., New York.

Crandall, Judith A. 1987. *How to Write Tutorial Documentation*. Prentice Hall, Inc., Englewood Cliffs, NJ.

de Beaugrande, Robert. 1980. *Text, Discourse and Process*. Ablex Publishing Corporation.

de Cervantes, Miguel. 1981. Don Quixote de la Mancha. Translated [1700–1703] by Peter Anthony Motteux, Modern Giant Library edition.

DeJong, Gerald F. and Raymond F. Mooney. 1986. Explanation-based learning: An alternative view. *Machine Learning*, 1:145–176.

Doheny-Farina, Stephen, editor. 1988. *Effective Documentation: What we have learned from Research*. The MIT Press series in information systems. MIT Press.

Doyle, Jon and Ramesh S. Patil. 1991. Two theses of Knowledge Representation: Language restrictions, taxonomic classification, and the utility of representation devices. *Artificial Intelligence*, 48:261–297.

Duffy, T. M., T. E. Curran, and D. Sass. 1983. Documentation Design for Technical Job Tasks. *Human Factors*, 25(2):143–160.

Duin, Ann Hill. 1990. Computer Documentation – Centering on the Learner. *Journal of Computer-Based Instruction*, 17(2):73–78, Spring.

Elhadad, Michael, Steve Feiner, Kathleen McKeown, and Doree Seligmann. 1991. Generating Customized Text and Graphics in the COMET Explanation Testbed. In *Proceedings 1991 Winter Simulation Conference*, pages 1058–1065, Phoenix, Arizona, December 8-11.

Engelmann, Siegfried and Douglas Carnine. 1982. *Theory of Instruction: Principles and Applications*. Irvington Publishers, Inc., New York.

Erasmus, Desiderius. 1979. Collected works. James K. McConica et al.

Feiner, Steven K. and Kathleen R. McKeown. 1991. Automating the generation of coordinated multi-media explanations. *Computer*, 24(10):33–42, October.

Feldman, Katherine Voerwerk. 1972. The effects of the number of positive and negative instances, concept definitions, and emphasis of relevant attributes on the attainment of mathematical concepts. In *Proceedings of the Annual Meeting of the American Educational Research Association*, Chicago, Illinois.

Feldman, Katherine Voerwerk and Herbert J. Klausmeier. 1974. The effects of two kinds of definitions on the concept attainment of fourth- and eighth-grade students. *Journal of Educational Research*, 67(5):219–223, January.

Fikes, Richard E. and Nils J. Nilsson. 1990. STRIPS: A New Approach to the Application of Theorem Proving to Problem Solving. In James Allen, James Hendler, and Austin Tate, editors, *Readings in Planning*. Morgan Kaufmann Publishers, Inc., San Mateo, CA., pages 88–98.

Forbus, Kenneth D. and Johan de Kleer. 1993. *Building problem solvers*. MIT Press, Cambridge, MA.

Française, Académie. 1694. *Dictionnaire de l'Academie Française*. Veuve de Jean Baptiste Coignard, Paris.

Frasson, Claude and Gilles Gauthier, editors. 1990. *Intelligent Tutoring Systems: At the Crossroads of Artificial Intelligence and Education*. Ablex Publishing Corporation, Norwood, NJ.

Frederiksen, Norman. 1984. Implications of Cognitive Theory for Instruction in Problem Solving. *Journal of the Review of Educational Research*, 54(3):363–407, Fall.

Friedman, Daniel P. and Matthias Fellesisen. 1987. *The Little LISPer*. MIT Press, Cambridge, MA.

George, D. G., H. W. Mewes, and H. Kihara. 1987. A standardized format for sequence data exchange. *Protein Sequence and Data Analysis*, 1(1):27–39.

Gick, Mary L. and Keith J. Holyoak. 1980. Analogical Problem Solving. *Cognitive Psychology*, 12:306–355.

Gil, Yolanda. 1994. Knowledge refinement in a reflective architecture. In *Proceedings of AAAI-94*, pages 520–526, Seattle, WA. AAAI, AAAI/MIT Press.

Gillingham, Mark G. 1988. Text in Computer-Based Instruction: What the Research Says. *Journal of Computer-Based Instruction*, 15(1):1–6, Winter.

Giora, Rachel. 1988. On the informativeness requirement. *Journal of Pragmatics*, 12:547–565.

Gold, E. Mark. 1965. *Models of Goal-Seeking and Learning*. Ph.D. thesis, University of California, Los Angeles, CA., January.

Gold, E. Mark. 1967. Language Identification in the Limit. *Information and Control*, 10:447–474.

Greenwald, John. 1984. How does this #%$! Thing Work? *Time*, June. (page 64, Week of June 18, 1984).

Hammond, Kristian J. 1990. Explaining and Repairing Plans that Fail. *Artificial Intelligence*, 45(1-2):173–229, September.

Harbison, Samuel P. and Guy L. Steele. 1993. *C: A Reference Manual*. Prentice Hall.

Hastings, G. Prentice and Kathryn J. King. 1986. *Creating Effective Documentation for Computer Programs*. Prentice-Hall.

Holland, John H., Keith J. Holyoak, Richard E. Nisbett, and Paul R. Thagard. 1987. *Induction: Processes of Inference, Learning and Discovery*. Computational Models of Cognition and Perception. The MIT Press, Cambridge, MA.

Horton, William K. 1991. *Illustrating Computer Documentation: The Art of Presenting Information Graphically and Online*. John Wiley and Sons, Inc., New York.

Houtz, John C., J. William Moore, and J. Kent Davis. 1973. Effects of Different Types of Positive and Negative Examples in Learning "non-dimensioned" Concepts. *Journal of Educational Psychology*, 64(2):206–211.

Hovy, Eduard and Marie Meteer, editors. 1990. *Proceedings of the AAAI Workshop on Evaluating Natural Language Generators*. AAAI, Boston, MA.

Hovy, Eduard H., Julia L. Lavid, Elisabeth Maier, Vibhu O. Mittal, and Cécile L. Paris. 1992. Employing Knowledge Resources in a New Text Planner Architecture. In Robert Dale, Eduard Hovy, Dietmar Rösner, and Oliviero Stock, editors, *Aspects of Automated Natural Language Generation*. Springer-Verlag, Berlin, pages 57–73.

Kambhampati, Subbarao. 1990a. A Theory of Plan Modification. In *Proceedings of the Eighth National Conference on Artificial Intelligence*, pages 177–182, Boston, MA, July.

Kambhampati, Subbarao. 1990b. Mapping and Retrieval During Plan Reuse: A Validation Structure Based Approach. In *Proceedings of the Eighth National Conference on Artificial Intelligence*, pages 170–176, Boston, MA, July.

Keene, Sonya E. 1989. *Object-Oriented Programming in Common Lisp*. Addison-Wesley Publishing Co., Reading, MA.

Klausmeier, Herbert J. 1976. Instructional Design and the Teaching of Concepts. In J. R. Levin and V. L. Allen, editors, *Cognitive Learning in Children*. Academic Press, New York.

Klausmeier, Herbert J. and Katherine Voerwerk Feldman. 1975. Effects of a Definition and a Varying Number of Examples and Non-Examples on Concept Attainment. *Journal of Educational Psychology*, 67(2):174–178.

Klausmeier, Herbert J., E. S. Ghatala, and D. A. Frayer. 1974. *Conceptual Learning and Development, a Cognitive View*. Academic Press, New York.

Knuth, Donald E. 1979. *TₑX and MetaFont: New Directions in Typesetting*. Digital Press, Bedford, MA.

Knuth, Donald E. 1990. *The TₑXbook*. Addison-Wesley Publishing Co., Reading, MA.

Kozma, Robert B. 1991. The Impact of Computer-Based Tools and Embedded Prompts on Writing Processes and Products of Novice and Advanced College Writers. *Cognition and Instruction*, 8(1):1–27.

Kukich, Karen. 1983. *Knowledge-Based Report Generation: A Knowledge-Engineering Approach to Natural Language Report Generation*. Ph.D. thesis, University of Pittsburgh.

LeFevre, Jo-Anne and Peter Dixon. 1986. Do Written Instructions Need Examples? *Cognition and Instruction*, 3(1):1–30.

Ling, Xiaofeng. 1991. Inductive Learning from Good Examples. In *Proceedings of the Twelfth International Joint Conference on Artificial Intelligence (IJCAI 91)*, pages 751–756, Sydney, Australia, August.

Lisp Users Group. 1984. Programming in Lisp: Local Users Guide (1984). Technical Documentation, University of Southern California. Los Angeles, CA.

Litchfield, Brenda C., Marcy P. Driscoll, and John V. Dempsey. 1990. Presentation Sequence and Example Difficulty: Their Effect on Concept and Rule Learning in Computer-Based Instruction. *Journal of Computer-Based Instruction*, 17(1):35–40, Winter.

London, Robert. 1992. Student Modeling to Support Multiple Instructional Approaches. *User Modeling and User-Adapted Interaction*, 2(1–2):117–154.

Lucid, Inc. 1990. Lucid Advanced User's Guide. Hewlett-Packard Documentation for version 4.2.

Lyons, John D. 1989. *Exemplum: The Rhetoric of Example in Early Modern France and Italy*. Princeton University Press, Princeton, NJ.

MacGregor, Robert. 1988. A Deductive Pattern Matcher. In *Proceedings of the 1988 Conference on Artificial Intelligence*, St Paul, Mn, August. American Association of Artificial Intelligence.

MacGregor, Robert. 1991. The Evolving Technology of Classification-Based Knowledge Representation Systems. In John Sowa, editor, *Principles of Semantic Networks: Explorations in the Representation of Knowledge*. Morgan Kaufmann, San Mateo, CA.

MacLachlan, James. 1986. Psychologically Based Techniques for Improving Learning within Computerized Tutorials. *Journal of Computer-Based Instruction*, 13(3):65–70, Summer.

Mann, William C. and Sandra A. Thompson. 1988. Rhetorical Structure Theory: Towards a Functional Theory of Text Organization. *Text*, 8:243–281.

Markle, S. M. and P. W. Tiemann. 1969. *Really Understanding Concepts*. Stipes Press, Urbana, Illinois.

Maynard, John. 1982. A User-Driven Approach to Better Manuals. *IEEE Transactions on Professional Communication*, PC-25(41):216–219, March.

McCarthy, John, Paul W. Abrahams, Daniel J. Edwards, Timothy P. Hart, and Michael I. Levin. 1985. *LISP 1.5 Programmer's Manual*. The MIT Press, Cambridge, MA.

McGilton, Henry and Mary Campione. 1992. *Postscript by Example*. Addison-Wesley Publishing Co., Reading, MA.

Meehan, James R., editor. 1979. *UCI Lisp Manual*. Lawrence Erlbaum Associates, Hillsdale, NJ.

Mellish, Chris and Roger Evans. 1989. Natural Language Generation from Plans. *Journal of Computational Linguistics*, 15(4):233–249, December.

Merrill, M. David and Robert D. Tennyson. 1977. *Concept Teaching: An Instructional Design Guide*. Educational Technology, Englewood Cliffs, NJ.

Merrill, M. David and Robert D. Tennyson. 1978. Concept Classification and Classification Errors as a function of Relationships between Examples and Non-Examples. *Improving Human Performance Quarterly*, 7(4):351–364, Winter.

Michalski, Ryszard S. 1983. A Theory and Methodology of Inductive Learning. In R. S. Michalski, J. G. Carbonell, and T. M. Mitchell, editors, *Machine Learning: An Artificial Intelligence Approach*. Tioga Press, Palo Alto, CA.

Michener, Edwina Rissland. 1977. *Epistemology, Representation, Understanding and Interactive Exploration of Mathematical Theories*. Ph.D. thesis, Massachusetts Institute of Technology, Cambridge, MA., February.

Michener, Edwina Rissland. 1978. Understanding Understanding Mathematics. *Cognitive Science Journal*, 2(4):361–383.

Mitchell, Tom M., Richard M. Keller, and Smadar T. Kedar-Cabelli. 1986. Explanation-Based Generalization: A Unifying View. *Machine Learning*, 1:48–80.

Mitchell, Tom M., Paul E. Utgoff, and Ranan Banerji. 1983. Learning by Experimentation: Acquiring and Refining Problem-Solving Heuristics. In Ryszard S. Michalski, Jaime G. Carbonell, and Tom M. Mitchell, editors, *Machine Learning: An Artificial Intelligence Approach*. Tioga Publishing Co., Palo Alto, CA, chapter 6, pages 163–189.

Mittal, Vibhu O. and Cécile L. Paris. 1992. Finding and Using Analogies in Generating Natural Language Object Descriptions. In *Proceedings of the Fourteenth Annual Conference of The Cognitive Science Society*, pages 996–1002, Indianapolis, IN, August. Lawrence Erlbaum Associates.

Mittal, Vibhu O. and Cécile L. Paris. 1994. Generating Examples For Use in Tutorial Explanations: The Use of a Subsumption Based Classifier. In *Proceedings of the Eleventh European Conference on Artificial Intelligence (ECAI-94)*, pages 530–534, Amsterdam, August. John Wiley and Sons.

Mohd-Hashim, Fakhruldin, Neal P. Juster, and Alan de Pennington. 1994. A functional approach to redesign. *Engineering with Computers*, 10(3):125–139, October.

Moore, Johanna D. 1995. *Participating in Explanatory Dialogues: Interpreting and Responding to Questions in Context*. MIT Press, Cambridge, MA.

Moore, Johanna D. and Cécile L. Paris. 1988. Constructing Coherent Texts Using Rhetorical Relations. In *Proceedings of the Tenth Annual Conference of the Cognitive Science Society*. Cognitive Science Society, August.

Moore, Johanna D. and Cécile L. Paris. 1989. Planning text for advisory dialogues. In *Proceedings of the Twenty-Seventh Annual Meeting of the Association for Computational Linguistics*, pages 203–211, Vancouver, British Columbia, June.

Moore, Johanna D. and Cécile L. Paris. 1991. Discourse Structure for Explanatory Dialogues. Presented at the Fall AAAI Symposium on

Discourse Structure in Natural Language Understanding and Generation, November.

Moore, Johanna D. and Cécile L. Paris. 1992. Exploiting User Feedback to Compensate for the Unreliability of User Models. *User Model and User Adapted Interaction Journal*, 2(4). (Authors in alphabetical order).

Moore, Johanna D. and Cécile L. Paris. 1993. Planning Text for Advisory Dialogues: Capturing Intentional and Rhetorical Information. *Computational Linguistics*, 19(4):651–694, December.

Moore, Johanna D. and William R. Swartout. 1989. A Reactive Approach to Explanation. In *Proceedings of the Eleventh International Conference on Artificial Intelligence*, pages 1505–1510, Detroit, MI, August. IJCAI.

Moore, Joseph. 1986. Direct Instruction: A Model of Instructional Design. *Educational Psychology*, 6(3):201–229.

Morgan, Chris. 1980. "What's wrong with technical writing today?". *BYTE*, 7(12):294, December.

Mostow, Jack. 1989. Design by Derivational Analogy: Issues in the Automated Replay of Design Plans. *Artificial Intelligence Journal*, 40:119–184, September.

Musen, M. A., L. M. Fagan, D. M. Combs, and E. H. Shortliffe. 1988. Use of a Domain Model to Drive an Interactive Knowledge Editing Tool. *International Journal of Man-Machine Studies*, 26:105–121.

Neches, Robert, William Swartout, and Johanna Moore. 1985. Enhanced Maintenance and Explanation of Expert Systems through explicit models of their development. *IEEE Transactions on Software Engineering*, SE-11(11), November.

Norman, Donald. 1988. *The Psychology of Everyday Things*. Basic Books, New York.

Norvig, Peter. 1992. *Paradigms of Artificial Intelligence Programming*. Morgan Kaufmann Publishers, San Mateo, CA.

Novak, Jr. Gordon S. 1985. Lisp Programming Lecture Notes. Technical Report AI-TR-85-06, Artificial Intelligence Laboratory, The University of Texas at Austin.

Nwana, Hyacinth S. 1991. User Modelling and User Adapted Interaction in an Intelligent Tutoring System. *User Modeling and User-Adapted Interaction*, 1(1):1–32.

Pakin, Sandra and Associates, Inc. 1984. *Documentation Development Methodology: Techniques for Improved Communications*. Prentice-Hall, Inc., Englewood Cliffs, NJ.

Paris, Cécile L. 1988. Tailoring Object Descriptions to the User's Level of Expertise. *Computational Linguistics*, 14(3):64–78, September.

Paris, Cécile L. 1991. Generation and Explanation: Building an Explanation Facility for the Explainable Expert Systems Framework. In C. Paris, W. Swartout, and W. Mann, editors, *Natural Language Generation in Artificial Intelligence and Computational Linguistics*. Kluwer Academic Publishers, Boston/Dordrecht/London, pages 49–81.

Paris, Cécile L. 1993. *User Modelling in Text Generation*. Pinter Publishers, London.

Park, Ok-Choon and Robert D. Tennyson. 1980. Adaptive Design Strategies for Selecting Number and Presentation Order of Examples in Coordinate Concept Acquisition. *Journal of Educational Psychology*, 72(3):362–370.

Park, Ok-Choon and Robert D. Tennyson. 1986. Computer-Based Response-Sensitive Design Strategies for Selecting Presentation Form and Sequence of Examples in Learning of Coordinate Concepts. *Journal of Educational Psychology*, 78(2):153–158.

Patil, Ramesh S. 1993. Personal communication, July.

Perry, Greg. 1992. *C by Example*. McGraw Press: Osborne.

Pirolli, Peter. 1991. Effects of Examples and Their Explanations in a Lesson on Recursion: A Production System Analysis. *Cognition and Instruction*, 8(3):207–259.

Pirolli, Peter L. and John R. Anderson. 1985. The Role of Learning from Examples in the Acquisition of Recursive Programming Skills. *Canadian Journal of Psychology*, 39:240–272.

Pólya, George. 1945. *How to Solve it – A New Aspect of Mathematical Method*. Princeton University Press, Princeton, New Jersey.

Pólya, George. 1973. *Induction and Analogy in Mathematics*, volume 1 of *Mathematics and Plausible Reasoning*. Princeton University Press, Princeton, NJ.

Reder, Lynne M., Davida H. Charney, and Kim I. Morgan. 1986. The Role of Elaborations in learning a skill from an Instructional Text. *Memory and Cognition*, 14(1):64–78.

Reed, S. K., A. Dempster, and M. Ettinger. 1985. Usefulness of Analogous Solutions for Solving Algebra Word Problems. *Journal of Experimental Psychology: Learning, Memory and Cognition*, 11:106–125.

Reed, S. K., G. W. Ernst, and R. Banerji. 1974. The Role of Analogy in Transfer between Similar Problem States. *Cognitive Psychology*, 6:436–450.

Reiser, Brian J., John R. Anderson, and Robert G. Farrell. 1985. Dynamic Student Modelling in an Intelligent Tutor for Lisp Programming. In *Proceedings of the Ninth International Conference on Artificial Intelligence*, pages 8–14. IJCAI-85 (Los Angeles).

Reisner, P. 1981. Formal grammar and human factors design of an interactive graphics system. *IEEE Transactions on Software Engineering*, SE-7(2):229–240.

Rissland, Edwina L. 1978. The Structure of Mathematical Knowledge. Technical Report 472, Massachusetts Institute of Technology – Artificial Intelligence Laboratory, Cambridge, MA., August.

Rissland, Edwina L. 1980. Example Generation. In *Proceedings of the Third National Conference of the Canadian Society for Computational Studies of Intelligence*, pages 280–288. CIPS, Toronto, Ontario, May.

Rissland, Edwina L. 1981. Constrained Example Generation. COINS Technical Report 81-24, Department of Computer and Information Science, University of Massachusetts, Amherst, MA.

Rissland, Edwina L. 1983. Examples in Legal Reasoning: Legal Hypotheticals. In *Proceedings of the International Joint Conference on Artificial Intelligence*, pages 90–93, Karlsruhe, Germany. IJCAI.

Rissland, Edwina L. and Kevin D. Ashley. 1986. Hypotheticals as Heuristic Device. In *Proceedings of the National Conference on Artificial Intelligence*, pages 289–297. AAAI.

Rissland, Edwina L. and Elliot M. Soloway. 1980. Overview of an Example Generation System. In *Proceedings of the National Conference on Artificial Intelligence*, pages 256–258. AAAI.

Rissland, Edwina L., Eduardo M. Valcarce, and Kevin D. Ashley. 1984. Explaining and Arguing with Examples. In *Proceedings of the National Conference on Artificial Intelligence*, pages 288–294. AAAI, August.

Rivest, Ron L. and Robert Sloan. 1988. Learning Complicated Concepts Reliably and Usefully. In *Proceedings of the Workshop on Computational Learning Theory*, Pittsburgh, PA.

Robertson, Ian and Hank Kahney. 1996. The use of examples in expository texts: Outline of an interpretation theory for text analysis. *Instructional Science*, 24(2):93–123.

Roth, S., J. Mattis, and X. Mesnard. 1991. Graphics and Natural Language as Components of Automatic Explanation. In *Intelligent User Interfaces*. Addison-Wesley, Reading, MA, pages 207–239.

Roth, Steven F. and William E. Hefley. 1993. Intelligent Multimedia Presentation Systems: Research and Principles. In *Intelligent Multimedia Interfaces*. AAAI/MIT Press, Menlo Park, CA, pages 13–59.

UNIX Documentation. 1986. UNIX User's Reference Manual 4.3 Berkeley Software Distribution. Computer Systems Research Group, Computer Science Division, University of California, Berkeley, CA.

Schank, Roger C. and Christopher K. Riesbeck. 1981. *Inside Computer Understanding: Five Programs plus miniatures*. Lawrence Erlbaum Associates, Hillsdale, NJ.

Schneider, M. L. 1982. Models for the Design of Static Software User Assistance. In Albert Badre and Ben Shneiderman, editors, *Directions in Human/Computer Interaction*. Ablex Publishing Co., Norwood, NJ, pages 137–148.

Shapiro, Ehud Y. 1983. *Algorithmic Program Debugging*. The MIT Press, Cambridge, MA. (ACM Distinguished Doctoral Dissertation).

Shapiro, Stuart C. 1986. *LISP: An Interactive Approach*. Computer Science Press, Rockville, MD.

Simpson, Henry and Steven M. Casey. 1988. *Developing Effective User Documentation: A Human Factors Approach.* McGraw-Hill, Englewood Cliffs, NJ.

Sleeman, Derek and John Seely Brown, editors. 1982. *Intelligent Tutoring Systems.* Academic Press, Inc.

Stanfill, Craig and David Waltz. 1986. Toward Memory-Based Reasoning. *Communications of the ACM*, 29(12):1213–1228, December.

Steele Jr., Guy L. 1984. *Common Lisp: The Language.* Digital Press.

Stevens, W. Richard. 1990. *UNIX: Network Programming.* Prentice Hall, Englewood Cliffs, NJ.

Stuart, Ann. 1984. *Writing and Analyzing Effective Computer System Documentation.* Holt, Rinehart, and Winston.

Suthers, Daniel D. and Edwina L. Rissland. 1988. Constraint Manipulation for Example Generation. COINS Technical Report 88-71, Computer and Information Science, University of Massachusetts, Amherst, MA.

Swartout, William and Stephen Smoliar. 1987. Explaining the link between causal reasoning and expert behaviour. In *Proceedings of the Symposium on Computer Applications in Medical Care*, Washington, DC., November. Also appears in "Topics in Medical Artificial Intelligence," Miller, P.L. (editor), Springer-Verlag.

Swartout, William R. 1983. The GIST behavior explainer. In *Proceedings of the National Conference on Artificial Intelligence, AAAI*, Washington DC.

Swartout, William R., Cecile L. Paris, and Johanna D. Moore. 1992. Design for Explainable Expert Systems. *IEEE Expert*, 6(3):58–64.

Sweller, John and Graham A. Cooper. 1985. The Use of Worked Examples as a Substitute for Problem Solving in Learning Algebra. *Cognition and Instruction*, 2(1):59–89.

Tatar, Deborah G. 1987. *A Programmer's Guide to COMMON LISP.* Digital Press.

Tennyson, R. D., J. N. Chao, and J. Youngers. 1981. Concept Learning Effectiveness Using Prototype and Skill Development Presentation Forms. *Journal of Educational Psychology*, 73:326–334.

Tennyson, R. D., J. Youngers, and P. Suebsonthi. 1983. Concept Learning by Children using Instructional Presentation Forms for Prototype Formation and Classification Skill Development. *Journal of Educational Psychology*, 75:280–291.

Tennyson, Robert D. and Ok-Choon Park. 1980. The Teaching of Concepts: A Review of Instructional Design Research Literature. *Review of Educational Research*, 50(1):55–70, Spring.

Tennyson, Robert D., M. Steve, and R. Boutwell. 1975. Instance Sequence and Analysis of Instance Attribute Representation in Concept Acquisition. *Journal of Educational Psychology*, 67:821–827.

Tennyson, Robert D. and C. L. Tennyson. 1975. Rule Acquisition Design Strategy Variables: Degree of Instance Divergence, Sequence and Instance Analysis. *Journal of Educational Psychology*, 67:852–859.

Tennyson, Robert D., F. R. Wooley, and M. David Merrill. 1972. Exemplar and Non-Exemplar Variables which Produce Correct Classification Behaviour and Specified Classification Errors. *Journal of Educational Psychology*, 63:144–162.

Tinker, M. A. 1963. *Legibility of Print*. Iowa State University Press, Ames, IA.

Touretzky, David S. 1984. *LISP: A Gentle Introduction to Symbolic Computation*. Harper & Row Publishers, New York.

Trimble, Louis. 1985. *English for Science and Technology. A Discourse Approach*. Cambridge University Press, Cambridge.

Valiant, Leslie G. 1984. A Theory of the Learnable. *Communications of the ACM*, 27:1134–1142.

VanLehn, Kurt. 1987. Learning one Subprocedure per Lesson. *Artificial Intelligence*, 31(1):1–40, January.

Veloso, Manuela M. and Jaime G. Carbonell. 1990. Derivational Analogy in PRODIGY: Automating Case Acquistion, Storage and Utilization. Working Manuscript, School for Computer Science, Carnegie-Mellon University.

Vetterling, William T., William H. Press, Saul A. Teukolsky, and Brian P. Flannery. 1990. *Numerical Recipes Example Book (C)*. Cambridge University Press, Cambridge, MA.

Wahlster, Wolfgang, Elisabeth Andre, W. Finkler, H. J. Profitlich, and Thomas Rist. 1993. Plan-based integration of natural-language and graphics generation. *Artificial Intelligence*, 63(12):387–427, October.

Wahlster, Wolfgang, Elisabeth André, Winfried Graf, and Thomas Rist. 1991. Designing Illustrated Texts: How Language Production is Influenced by Graphics Generation. In *Proc. European Chapter of the Assoc. for Computational Linguistics*, pages 8–14, Berlin, April.

Waite, Mitchell, Donald Martin, and Stephen Prata. 1983. UNIX *Primer Plus*. Howard W. Sams and Co., Inc., Indianapolis, IN.

Ward, Mark and John Sweller. 1990. Structuring Effective Worked Examples. *Cognition and Instruction*, 7(1):1–39.

Webster, Merriam. 1997. The merriam webster dictionary. Macmillan Publishers.

Weinberg, Bernard. 1961. *History of Literary Criticism in the Italian Renaissance*. University of Chicago Press, Chicago, IL.

Werth, Paul. 1984. *Focus, Coherence and Emphasis*. Croom Helm, London, England.

Wile, David S., 1987. *POPART: Producer of Parsers and Related Tools – System Builders' Manual*. USC/Information Sciences Institute, Marina del Rey, CA.

Wilensky, Robert. 1983. *Planning and Understanding: A Computational Approach to Human Reasoning*. Addison-Wesley Publishing Company, Reading, MA.

Wilensky, Robert. 1986. *Common LISPcraft*. W. W. Norton and Co., New York.

Williams, P. W. 1977. Quote from the Comptroller-General of the United States. New Scientist, December.

Willows, Dale M. and Harvey A. Houghton, editors. 1987a. *The Psychology of Illustration*, volume 1. (Basic Research). Springer-Verlag, New York.

Willows, Dale M. and Harvey A. Houghton, editors. 1987b. *The Psychology of Illustration*, volume 2. (Instructional Issues). Springer-Verlag, New York.

Winston, Patrick H., Thomas O. Binford, Boris Katz, and Michael Lowry. 1983. Learning Physical Description from Functional Definitions, Examples and Precedents. Technical Report STAN-CS-82-950, Artificial Intelligence Laboratory, Stanford University, January. Also numbered AIM-349.

Winston, Patrick Henry. 1975. Learning Structural Descriptions from Examples. In Patrick Henry Winston, editor, *The Psychology of Computer Vision*. McGraw Hill, New York, chapter 5, pages 158–209.

Winston, Patrick Henry and Berthold Klaus Paul Horn. 1984. *LISP*. Addison-Wesley, Reading, MA.

Woolf, Beverly and David D. McDonald. 1984a. Building a Computer Tutor: Design Issues. *IEEE Computer*, pages 61–73, September.

Woolf, Beverly and David D. McDonald. 1984b. Context-Dependent Transitions in Tutoring Discourse. In *Proceedings of the Third National Conference on Artificial Intelligence*, pages 355–361. AAAI.

Woolf, Beverly and Tom Murray. 1987. A Framework for Representing Tutorial Discourse. In *Proceedings of the Tenth International Joint Conference on Artificial Intelligence*, pages 189–192. IJCAI.

Woolf, Beverly Park. 1991. Representing, Acquiring, and Reasoning about Tutoring Knowledge. In R. Lewis and S. Otsuki, editors, *Advanced Research on Computers in Education*. Elsevier Science Publishers B.V. (North-Holland), pages 39–48.

Woolf, Beverly Park, Daniel Suthers, and Tom Murray. 1988. Discourse Control for Tutoring: Case Studies in Example Generation. COINS Technical Report 88-49, Computer and Information Science, University of Massachusetts.

Yoder, Cornelia Marie. 1986. *An Expert System for Providing On-Line Information Based Upon Knowledge of Individual User Characteristics.* Ph.D. thesis, Syracuse University, August.

Zhu, Xinming and Herbert A. Simon. 1987. Learning Mathematics from Examples and by Doing. *Cognition and Instruction*, 4(3):137–166.

Appendix A

Some Descriptions of a LIST

During the initial stages of this work, we conducted an extensive analysis of programming language descriptions, in a variety of books intended for a variety of user types. In order to illustrate how widely some of these descriptions vary, and in an effort to illustrate how well our system can generate descriptions, we present several descriptions of a `list` in LISP (the data-structure, and not the function-call), from various books, and point out some of their strengths and weaknesses, which served as useful input to the system.

A.1 Description 1

Now we are ready to perform an operation in LISP. LISP accepts commands in a somewhat different form from most calculators. First, we begin with a parenthesis. Next, we specify the name of the operation we would like to perform. Then we give the arguments we would like to use. We finish off the whole thing with a final parenthesis. For example, if we want to compute "8 + 3" using LISP, we type the following:

```
--> (+ 8 3)
11
```

[Description of arithmetic operators and prefix notation deleted]

For example, if we want to multiply 8 by 3, we can type:

```
--> (* 8 3)
24
```

LISP programmers sometimes call these commands *s-expressions*.

[Description of LISP's suitability for symbolic computation deleted]

The symbolic expressions given above are also called lists. A list is a sequence of objects inside a pair of parentheses.

From (Wilensky, 1986), p. 3.

Analysis: This description of a list is clearly not intended for intro-ductory users. Not only does the author not define/introduce the con-cept before presenting examples, but the examples of the *data-structure* list, are presented as an aside while introducing *functions* (arithmetic operations that happen to be lists). These examples of function calls are then used to illustrate the definition of a list. The definition itself is not well integrated with the examples, with the two examples occur-ring on two different (successive) pages, and the definition occurring two paragraphs after the second example.

A.2 Description 2

LISP data-structures are called *s-expressions*. An s-expression is:

1. a number, e.g., 15, written as an optional plus or minus sign, followed by one or more digits.

2. a symbol, e.g., FOO, written as a letter followed by zero or more letters or digits.

3. a string, e.g., "This is a string", written as a double quote,

followed by zero or more characters, followed by another double quote.

4. a character, e.g., #
   q, written as a sharp sign, followed by another backslash, followed by a character.

5. a list of s-expressions, e.g., (A B) or (IS TALL (FATHER BILL)), written as a left parenthesis, followed by zero or more s-expressions, followed by a right parenthesis.

From (Charniak et al., 1987), p. 2.

Analysis: This description of a list presents two examples of a list before the definition. Both the examples contain only symbols. The second example contains a sublist, but that is not explained or mentioned in the explanation.

A.3 Description 3

S-Expressions (*symbolic expressions*): these are defined recursively as follows:

- An atom is an S-Expression
- If x_1 ... x_n are S-Expressions, then $(x_1 ... x_n)$, called a list of x_1 ... x_n, is an S-Expression

Examples:

```
(ONTOGENY)
(THIS IS A LIST)
(* PI (EXPT R 2))
(ALL X (IF (MAN X) (MORTAL X)))
()        ((()))       ((()())())
```

The empty list, () is equivalent to the special atom NIL.

From (Lisp Users Group, 1984), p. 14.

Analysis: This description of a list occurs as part of a description of an S-Expression. There are a number of examples following the definition. The first two examples illustrate the variability in number of data elements, and the others illustrate the variability in the type of data elements. The examples do not illustrate one feature at a time (the third example illustrates that elements can be characters or lists, in addition to symbols, however, there is no prompt). The fifth example contains three lists in one line, of an empty list and combinations of empty lists. The order of presentation of the examples is not in terms of syntactic complexity, if it had been, the empty list would have been presented first.

A.4   Description 4

The most common kind of S-Expression is the list. A definition of a list is: *A left parenthesis followed by zero or more S-Expressions followed by a right parenthesis is a list.*   Of course lists, as well as atoms, are themselves S-expressions, so (A (B C) D) is a list as well as (A B C D). We refer to the S-expressions in a list as *elements* or *members* of the list. The most important list is the one with no members — ( ), called the *empty list* or the *null list*. Some more lists are shown below:

```
( )
(ATOM)
(ALPHA BETA GAMMA)
(5 IS A NUMBER
   "THIS IS A STRING")
((A LIST WITHIN A LIST))
( ( ) )
(((((( )))))
(AN (INTERESTING
     ((LIST) STRUCTURE)))
```

From (Shapiro, 1986), p. 8.

Analysis: This description presents two examples of relatively complex lists with the definition. After some elaboration, more examples of lists are presented. These examples are well structured and in order of increasing syntactic complexity. Unfortunately, there are no prompts, even when the third example introduces two new data types, or for the recursive cases. The anomalous example, of the symbol NIL being a list is not introduced, even though the empty list is explicitly discussed in the definition.

A.5 Description 5

A list looks like a sequence of objects, without commas between them, enclosed in parentheses:

```
(tables chairs lamps bookcases)
```

The parentheses identify a unit, and that unit can be used for a variety of purposes. In fact, lists provide both aprimary way of storing data and the means for defining and calling functions.

A list can have any number and kind of elements, including other lists. A list can be as deeply nested as you wish. A list can also have no elements, in which case it is represented as NIL, and may be written as "( )" or "NIL". These two forms are completely interchangeable. NIL is a special symbol, whose print name is "NIL" and whose value is always NIL. Table 2-2 contains simple lists made up of kinds of elements you have already seen. Lists can also combine different kinds of elements, as shown in Table 2-3.

These lists can be considered ways to store data. For example, you might want to store your inventory as a list, or group together names and phone numbers in a list of lists. Appropriately constructed lists can also be used to call functions in LISP. If you type any of the lists in Table 2-4 to LISP, you will get an appropriate response.

[15 lines on using lists as functions deleted here]

TABLE 2-2. Some possible lists:

(1 2 3 4 5)	a list of numbers
(A B C D)	a list of symbols
(#\A #\B #\C #\D)	a list of characters
(this is a list)	a list of symbols

TABLE 2-3. More complex lists:

(this is (also) a list)	a list whose third element is a list
((12 eggs (large))	a list of lists of numbers, symbols
(1 bread (whole wheat))	and lists
(4 pizzas (frozen with anchovies)))	
("this is a string in a list" -53)	a list of a string and a number
((beth "555-5834") (pat "555-8098"))	a list containing two lists

TABLE 2-4. Lists that can be used to call functions:

(SQRT 2)	a list whose first element is the name of a function
(+ 2 3)	a list whose first element is the name of a function
(- 6 5 4)	a list whose first element is the name of a function

From (Tatar, 1987), p. 16.

Analysis: The examples presented in this description are collected into groups of four (thus, although the total number of examples is quite large, as suggested by Clark (1971), they are partitioned into smaller groups of four each). The examples and the groups are ordered by complexity. They also contain prompts about the features being illustrated in the examples. Only the second example in the second group of more complex examples is out of sequence (and has an ambiguous prompt: a user might conceivably be led to think that the data-elements were lists that contained only numbers, symbols and sub-lists in that example). In the third table, the examples are again ordered by complexity (the number of elements increases). This is a good description of a list for naive users. Its only drawback is that the examples themselves are not well-integrated within the text; however, the text refers to them explicitly.

A.6 Description 6

When left and right parentheses surround something, we call the result a *list*, and speak of its *elements*. In our very first example, the list (+ 3.14 2.71) has three elements, +, 3.14, and 2.71.

[Discussion on the prefix notation deleted]

- Indivisible things like 27, 3.14 and +, as well as things like FOO, B27 and HYPHENATED-SYMBOL are called *atoms*.

- Atoms like 27 and 3.14 are called *numeric* atoms, or numbers.

- Atoms like FOO, B27, HYPHENATED-SYMBOL, FIRST and + are called *symbolic* atoms, or symbols.

- A *list* consists of a left parenthesis, followed by zero or more atoms or lists, followed by a right parenthesis.

From (Winston and Horn, 1984), p. 20.

Analysis: This description is somewhat confusing when taken out of the larger context in the book. However, it is clear that this description attempts to reinforce the definition of a list by presenting it twice, once initially, with examples, and then, once again, in a group with other data-types.

If the two parts of the description of list are considered separately, there are several concerns that may be raised about the first half: only one example is presented; this happens to be a potentially confusing one (the first element of the example list is the "+" symbol, a special symbol in Lisp, and almost always used as the name for the addition function, rather than a variable name). The single example also does not illustrate any of the other features of a list.

In the second attempt to describe a list, following shortly afterwards, the description of a list occurs along with descriptions of other data-types in Lisp. However, even though the other data-types are illustrated with examples, the description of a list does not contain any examples. It would seem that the goal to describe a list (in this book) is subsumed by some other goal (possibly the goal to describe arithmetic operations).

A.7 Description 7

A list always begins with a left parenthesis. Then come zero or more pieces of data (called the elements of a list) and a right parenthesis. Some examples of lists are:

```
(AARDVARK)
(RED YELLOW GREEN BLUE)
(2 3 5 11 19)
(3 FRENCH FRIES)
```

A list may contain other lists as elements. Given the three lists:

```
(BLUE SKY) (GREEN GRASS) (BROWN EARTH)
```

we can make a list by combining them all with a parentheses.

```
((BLUE SKY) (GREEN GRASS) (BROWN EARTH))
```

From (Touretzky, 1984), p. 35.

Analysis: This description will be familiar to the reader, as a model description, similar to the ones that the system generates. It presents the definition, followed by examples illustrating the variable features of a list. The recursive example is prefaced by additional explanation, and the examples are well-integrated with the text. (There are two differences between the system generated descriptions and this one: the system descriptions often generate lists with the same elements, thus repeating certain data-elements, and the symbols in the lists do not necessarily possess any meaning, unlike the lists here: "blue sky" and "3 french fries".)

Appendix B

The Heuristics Used in the System

There are a number of heuristics used in the system to decide on different decisions. Many of these heuristics depend on the text type being generated. Because the current implementation does not handle intermediate texts, the heuristics listed here deal only with the introductory and the advanced texts:

- **when should an example be generated:**
  - if the text is introductory, and the concept definition has been presented, generate examples to illustrate the definition
  - if the text is advanced, examples should not be presented until the complete description of the concept has been presented textually

- **information in text, examples, and both text and examples:**
  - if the text type is introductory:
    * the definition of the concept must be described textually
    * information on different types of elements in an concept can be conveyed using only examples

* information on recursive element types (such as lists of other lists) must be conveyed through both text and examples

- if the text type is advanced:

  * all of the information should be communicated in the text
  * the syntactic information can be conveyed through examples as well (but there is no replacement of textual elaboration by the examples)

- **characteristics of the textual explanation:**

  - if the text is introductory:

    * the textual explanation should be about the syntactic construction
    * anomalous cases should not be introduced in the explanation

  - If the text is advanced, the textual explanation must be complete with regard to all the information represented about the concept.

- **characteristics of the examples:**

  - if the text is introductory:

    * the examples should introduce one feature at a time
    * the elements of the examples should be simple ones
    * anomalous examples should not be presented along with other positive examples
    * if an interesting negative example is available, the example should be presented, (along with an explanation of the differences between the negative example and the positive ones)
    * positive examples that differ in a variable feature should be presented to illustrate that variable feature
    * if a positive—negative pair of examples is presented to illustrate a critical feature, then the example pair should differ in only the critical feature

  - if the text is advanced:

* the examples should contain as many features as possible

* the elements of the examples can be as complex as necessary to illustrate the range of variation

* because the definition is complete, there should be no anomalous examples in this context). Negative examples are not presented

- **number of examples:**

  - if the text is introductory

    * the number of examples should be at least as many as the number of features to be introduced

    * if a recursive example needs to be presented, then there should be background examples that should be generated in addition for use in the recursive example

  - if the text is advanced, the number of examples is determined by the minimum number of examples that convey all the features. To illustrate variable features, at least two examples should be presented, and all of the variable features should be varied

- **order of example presentation:** examples should be presented ordered by complexity at both the feature level and the individual example level.

  - *ordering groups of examples illustrating a feature:* groups of examples illustrating a particular feature should be sequenced by the relative complexity of that feature

  - *ordering examples within each feature group:*

    * within a group, the examples should be ordered by the complexity of each example

    * between positive–negative pairs, the positive example should be presented before the negative example

    * if the negative example is an interesting negative example of another concept, then the positive negative pair should be presented after all the other regular (not anomalous) examples

    * anomalous examples should be presented after all other examples (including interesting negative examples).

- **position of the examples:**

  - if the text type is introductory, the examples illustrating a feature in a concept should be presented as part of the elaboration on that feature (after the feature is mentioned). This will result in examples interspersed within the explanation

  - if the text type is advanced, all examples should be presented after the complete explanation

- **when should prompts be generated:**

  - prompts should be generated when the example to be presented has more features than required by the discourse goal that caused the example to be generated

  - prompts should be generated when the example occurs far away from the point that the concept the example illustrates was described

  - prompts should be generated if the example is as a result of combining two communicative goals

  - if the text type is advanced and the example is recursive, prompts should be generated to mention that fact

Appendix C

Possible Extensions: A Knowledge Base Interface

Chapter 10 discusses some possible applications that the framework could be extended to. One of the extensions mentioned there was a browser or an interface for complex knowledge bases. This chapter describes some preliminary experiments to evaluate the advantages of such an approach. These experiments suggest that having a natural language-based interface, particularly one capable of generating descriptions that include relevant examples, can have significant advantages, in certain contexts or domains, over alternative techniques, particularly over the browsing and unaided modification of the actual specifications.

C.1 Debugging Complex Knowledge Bases

Knowledge base construction is often an iterative process of debugging and refinement. As knowledge bases (KBs) increase in size, the problems of detecting incorrect, inconsistent or incomplete specifications become increasingly difficult, especially for domain experts who may be unfamiliar with the knowledge representation language and its intricacies. To alleviate this problem, a number of previous efforts have considered approaches that would allow domain experts to inspect formal specifications using natural language (Gil, 1994; Swartout, 1983). However, as discussed in the initial chapters, several studies have shown that people can usually understand and verify specific examples more easily and quickly than abstract, textual descriptions (Reder, Charney, and Morgan, 1986; Pirolli, 1991).

The experiments described in this chapter extend the generation framework described in the preceding chapters with work on debugging from examples, for example (Shapiro, 1983; Mitchell, Utgoff, and Banerji, 1983), to design a novel interface to KBs. This interface allows users to inspect and debug KBs by identifying problems in automatically generated examples and accompanying natural language descriptions. Rather than examining the original, programmatic specification, (which can be both complex and confusing), users are presented with much simpler descriptions of the original specifications: the system splits apart the original specifications into much smaller "chunks of information" — which are then presented to the user as a combination of text and examples. Depending on the type of information to be presented, the system can present multiple examples to highlight specific aspects in the specification. Since the examples and text are generated automatically from the underlying KB specifications, problems in the original specifications show up as original specifications show up as problems in the text or examples. The user can then flag examples that seem problematic.

Using information about (1) the specific examples flagged by the user as being problematic, (2) information about the type of the problem (also specified by the user), and (3) the discourse plan underlying the automatically generated presentation, the system attempts to localize the problem in the KB specification. In cases where the system cannot uniquely identify the problem with the knowledge base, it generates additional descriptions for the expert to verify. This extension to the original framework integrates previous research in three areas: (1) knowledge acquisition and refinement (Gil, 1994; Musen et al., 1988), (2) reasoning about discourse plans (Moore and Paris, 1993), and (3) automatic example generation (Ashley and Aleven, 1992; Mittal and Paris, 1994). Based on our experiments, problems in the KB specification of a concept manifest themselves as a combination of one or more

of the following three types of errors in system generated explanations:
(1) incorrect examples, (2) incorrect explanations accompanying the examples, or (3) sequencing problems in the examples.

As discussed in chapter 5, the descriptions (and associated examples) are generated by a hierarchical discourse planner, which produces discourse plans recording the goals achieved by and the rhetorical relationships among plan components. When the user indicates that an example is incorrect (by highlighting the example), the system uses the discourse plan to generate and reason about hypotheses regarding possible errors in the KB specifications that could have led to the errors in the description generated. Thus, our system differs from previous work on example based debugging in machine learning (ML), as discussed, for instance, in (Shapiro, 1983; Mitchell, Utgoff, and Banerji, 1983), in that it uses knowledge about both the discourse plan, as well as domain specific knowledge, in order to identify possible problems in the KB.

To investigate the strengths and weaknesses of this approach in detecting and debugging KB problems, we looked at the different types of errors in descriptions that can indicate problems in the underlying KB, and how they can help in finding the problem. In order to minimize the extensions required to the original system, we attempted to conduct our experiments using a Backus-Naur Form (BNF) representation. This enables us to abstract away from system- and domain-specific representations, since BNF is a generic, domain- and task-neutral specification formalism that is capable of representing a wide variety of domains and tasks — including mechanical device design (Mohd-Hashim, Juster, and de Pennington, 1994), protein-structure mapping (George, Mewes, and Kihara, 1987) and interface requirements (Reisner, 1981). To further simplify the discussion, we use the same BNF fragment to illustrate the three types of errors that can occur in the automatically generated presentation. For this purpose, we use the specification of floating point numbers in Lisp, but the method discussed here is specific neither to Lisp, nor in fact to BNF. We have chosen this example here because (a) floating point numbers need no introduction, (b) the abstract specification of floating point numbers is sufficiently complex so as to illustrate the utility of examples, and (c) translating BNF to a KL-ONE style language such as LOOM was discussed in detail previously in chapter 5.

floating-point-number ::=

    [sign] {digit}* decimal-point {digit}+ [exponent]   *(1a)*

    | *[sign] {digit}+ [decimal-point {digit}*] exponent*   *(1b)*

sign ::= +|-   *(2)*

decimal-point ::= .   *(3)*

digit ::= *0 | 1 | 2 | 3 | 4 | 5 | 6 | 7 | 8 | 9*   *(4)*

exponent ::= *exponent-marker [sign] {digit}+*   *(5)*

exponent-marker ::= *e | s | f | d | l | E | S | F | D | L*   *(6)*

Figure C.1: Grammar fragment from (Steele, 1984, p.17)

C.2 Examples in Knowledge Acquisition

To illustrate how examples can help in detecting gaps in the KB, consider the grammar fragment shown in figure C.1 (the formal specification of floating point numbers in Lisp). Although this set of productions is one of the simpler ones in the grammar, it is easy to overlook some of the implications of the bracketing and the *kleene-* and *transitive-closures* in the productions. The rules are complex enough that a text-only paraphrase of the rules themselves may not be enough to spot a mistake in the representation. However, an example generated from *only* the faulty aspect can often stand out as a grossly wrong instance of the definition and can thus focus attention on specific aspects of abstract rules in a very effective fashion (Pirolli, 1991).

To generate and present the examples, the system must first determine the critical and variable features, in this case, of the concept FLOATING-POINT-NUMBER. In this case, the critical features are: (a) the presence of a decimal point accompanied by one or more digits on the right hand side of the decimal point, or (b) a number accompanied by an exponent. The variable features are: (a) the presence or absence of the sign, (b) the value of the sign, (c) the number of digits in the numbers, and (d) the values of the numbers. The system can now utilize this critical or variable categorization to generate sets of examples to

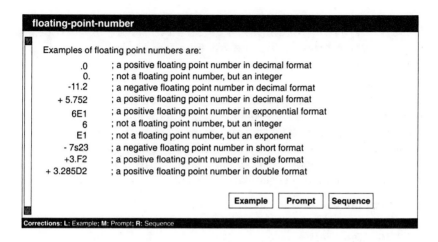

Figure C.2: Description for FLOATING-POINT-NUMBER.

effectively convey each of these attributes (critical attributes by pairs of almost identical positive-negative examples; variable attributes by groups of varying positive examples). The presentation order of the examples is determined by the relative complexity of each example. A typical output generated by the system is shown in figure C.2 (fragments of the discourse plan underlying the presentation of the critical features are shown in figure C.3).

Now suppose that the specification of the concept

FLOATING-POINT-NUMBER

is incorrect. The problems in the specification can manifest themselves in the resulting explanation that is generated in one of three ways: the examples generated by the system are incorrect, the explanations accompanying the examples are incorrect, or the examples are ordered in an inconsistent manner. (These can be marked by the domain expert as such by selecting the appropriate examples or prompts and using the buttons at the bottom of the screen.) In each of these cases, the system reasons about the underlying discourse plan used to generate the explanation in order to localize the potential cause of the problem.

Case 1. A wrong example is generated: There are two possible ways in which problems in the KB manifest themselves as incorrect examples in the resulting explanation:

Case 1.1. A simple wrong example: If the faulty example differs from its adjacent (correct) examples in only a single feature, the system can use this information in conjunction with the discourse plan to debug the KB specification. Consider, again, the specification of floating-point numbers in Lisp shown in figure C.1. The correct and one possible mistaken specification for rule (1a) are shown below:

floating-point-number ::=
   [sign] {digit}* decimal-point {digit}$^+$ [exponent] $\checkmark$
floating-point-number ::=
   [sign] {digit}* decimal-point {digit}* [exponent] $\times$

The resulting output generated by the system for the incorrect case is shown in figure C.4. The first and the third examples presented in the explanation are incorrect. It is clearly easier to spot the mistake in the individual examples than in the abstract specification.

Using our interface, the user can highlight these two items and indicate them as being incorrect examples of a floating point number. Based on this information, the system reasons as follows. First, it uses the discourse plan to determine what other examples in the presentation are most closely related to the items that were marked incorrect. The discourse plan indicates not only the examples that are related, but *how* they are related, e.g., whether they are contrastive examples for a critical feature, similar examples for a variable feature, and so on. In this case, the system determines that the first example was generated to illustrate the following variable features: the sign of the number, the number of digits on the left of the decimal point, the number of digits on the right of the decimal point, and the exponent. The second example was intended to highlight the variable nature of the digits *on the left* of the decimal point, and since that example was not marked wrong, the variable nature of the digits on the left of the decimal point is correct. The third example was supposed to illustrate the variable nature of the digits *on the right* of the decimal point, and that example was marked wrong. Since the other examples were not marked wrong, the system

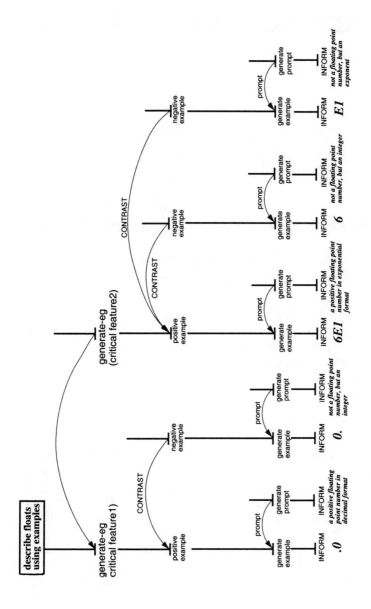

Figure C.3: Fragments of the discourse plan for the two critical features.

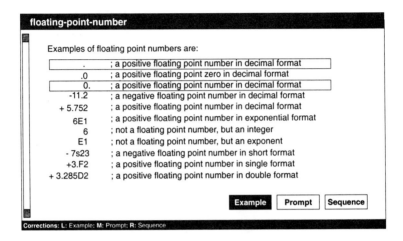

Figure C.4: A simple case of incorrect examples.

can, on the basis of the two wrong examples and the other correct examples, suggest a revision to the incorrect version of rule (1*a*). This revision regarding the optionality of digits on the right of the decimal point results in the transitive closure being modified to a kleene closure as follows:

floating-point-number ::=
 [*sign*] {*digit*}* *decimal-point* {*digit*}+ [*exponent*]

Case 1.2. A complex wrong example: in some cases, a component term used in the example (with its own critical and variable features) can be incorrect, making the larger example wrong. When an example containing such complex component terms is marked incorrect, the system can generate additional, simpler examples about the suspect component in order to localize the KB problem. Consider, for instance, the case in figure C.5. The fifth example in the sequence, which is also the first example where the exponent notation is used, is marked as incorrect by the user. The discourse plan indicates that the example in question was generated to illustrate the use of the exponent notation in rule (1*b*). The system examines the portion of the discourse plan

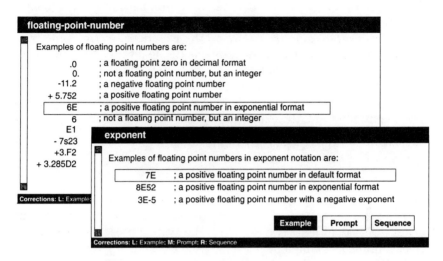

Figure C.5: A complex incorrect example can result in the generation of further examples.

regarding examples generated from rule (1*b*). Since one of the differences between the wrong example and its immediate neighbor is the exponent (the *[decimal-point {digit}*]* portion of the rule was not used in either of the two), the system can infer that the problem is in the specification of the exponent.

There are two other examples in the same explanation that also have exponents in them (the last two examples). These, however, use a different exponent markers ("F" and "D"). Thus, it is only possible to infer that *either the wrong marker was used, i.e., "E" is not allowed, or some other piece of information is missing*. To verify the first possibility, that "E" is an invalid exponent marker, the system generates another set of examples for floating point numbers that use the exponent marker "E" (shown in the lower half of figure C.5). In this case, the first example of an exponent is wrong. The system can now use the discourse structure used in generating the examples for the exponent to identify the problem. In this case, the difference between the first two examples of the exponent is that the second example has a positive number following the exponent marker whereas the first example does not. Thus, one possibility is that a positive number is necessary in these cases. The third example, which has a negative number after the exponent marker, allows the system to generalize the previous hypothesis (of needing a *positive* number following the exponent) to the hypothesis that any number, positive or negative, is needed. Since the production specified that the sign is optional, the only part of the production that could be wrong is about the optionality of the number. Thus, the system can suggest that the specification of the exponent be modified to make *both* the number and the exponent marker be required in all cases:

exponent ::= exponent-marker [sign] {digit}* $\qquad\qquad$ ✕

exponent ::= exponent-marker [sign] {digit}$^+$ $\qquad\qquad$ ✓

Case 2. A wrong prompt: Mistakes in the domain model can also result in the generation of incorrect textual prompts. Prompts can indicate errors in at least two cases: (a) the system presents a valid, positive example as being a negative, invalid example (or vice-versa), and (b) the system presents a valid example (either positive or negative), but the accompanying prompt (or explanation) is either irrelevant or inconsistent with the point being illustrated.

The first possibility can be handled in the same way as in case 1. However, the second possibility, where an invalid prompt is generated for a correct example, is often due to missing information, and must also be dealt with. For instance, consider the case where the system generates an example of a floating point number such as the one shown in figure C.6. If the specification of the production rule for the exponent, (rule 5) is faulty as given below:

exponent ::= [exponent-marker] [sign] {digit}$^+$ $\qquad\qquad$ ✕

The system would generate the example using the second production rule for floating point numbers — the part "5.7" from rule (1*b*), and the digits "5" and "2" from the faulty rule given above for the exponent. Also based on the faulty rule, the system would assume that the exponent-marker and the sign were optional and therefore not to be included initially. The resulting example generated is a valid floating point number "5.752", *but the accompanying textual prompt indicates that a mistake was made* in the specification. Selecting the prompt causes the system to generate additional examples for the same discourse goal that caused the generation of the example with the faulty

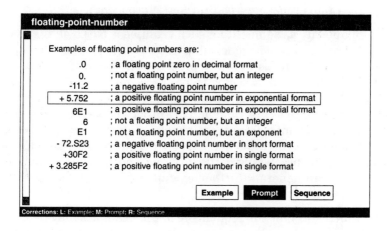

Figure C.6: Errors in prompts can indicate KB problems.

prompt in the first place. Exercising the different options of the production rule for the exponent, the system can infer that `exponent-marker` is not a variable feature, but a critical one (i.e., its presence is mandatory in the case of an exponent), and thus can propose the corrected rule:

$$exponent ::= exponent\text{-}marker\ [sign]\ \{digit\}^+ \qquad \checkmark$$

Case 3. A wrong presentation sequence: A third possible manifestation of KB problems can be seen in strange or surprising placement of examples (for instance, a simple example appearing after a number of complex examples of the same concept have been presented). In such cases, even though all the examples presented may be valid, the complexity assignment to each example is computed incorrectly because of the problems in the KB specifications. For instance, consider what happens if the bracketing of the transitive-closure term is done differently, as in the two rules:

$$floating\text{-}point\text{-}number ::=$$
$$[sign]\ \{digit\}^+\ [decimal\text{-}point\ \{digit\}^*\ ]\ exponent \qquad (1)$$

floating-point-number ::=

$\quad$ [*sign*] {*digit*}$^+$ [*decimal-point*] {*digit*}* *exponent* $\qquad$ (2)

The complexity assignment for each example is based on the number of productions involved in generating it. Thus, if rule (1) is used instead of rule (2), the examples would be presented in the order shown in figure C.7. Because +30F2 seems to be less complex than -72.S23, the user may highlight +30F2 and indicate that it is not in the expected sequence. The examples are valid and are otherwise sequenced correctly, so the system can infer from the discourse plan that the difference between the specification and the expected sequence of examples must be caused by the bracketing of the *[decimal-point]* {*digit*}* component. The system can generate further examples to verify this hypothesis with the domain expert.

This illustrates how the sequencing of the examples may help detect a problem even when all of the examples and their associated prompts are valid. Further work is required on some of these issues. It will be necessary to examine other domains as well to determine whether the KB inconsistencies that are identified via incorrect presentation sequences would typically also be manifest by either incorrect examples or incorrect prompts.

In cases where the expert selects more than one example as being faulty, the system examines the productions that were used in generating the faulty examples. If the productions have no terms in common, reasoning about each example is done independently, since the problems were probably due to entirely different reasons. Otherwise, the system engages in a clarification subdialogue for each common term.

C.3   Evaluation

The experimental system was implemented in the framework described in the preceding chapters; LOOM was used as the underlying knowledge representation system to implement the classification capabilities needed to determine the critical and variable features. The module for reasoning about possible inconsistencies was based on an assumption based truth maintenance system by Forbus and deKleer (1993). Although the system has been tested only on BNF representations of various domains, as noted previously, the BNF notation is not a severe

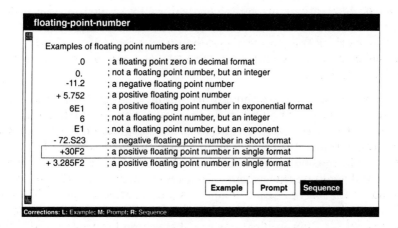

Figure C.7: Bad sequencing can also indicate KB problems.

limitation, because it is flexible enough to represent a large variety of domains ranging from mechanical design to protein structure.

As discussed at the beginning of this appendix, these experiments were not the major focus of our work, and as such were not evaluated rigorously. In an informal study with 16 subjects, we looked at users' abilities to find and pinpoint errors in KB specifications. We found that in almost all cases, all the subjects were able to detect *incorrect examples* such as the ones shown here (e.g., the floating point zero). In contrast, only 2 of the 16 users were able to find the corresponding errors by scrutinizing the (abstract) BNF definitions for 5 minutes. Similar results were found for cases when the examples were accompanied by *incorrect prompts*.

Unfortunately, our test participants had a more difficult time detecting KB problems that manifested themselves as *sequencing problems* in the presentation of examples. This is likely to be due to the fact that (a) finding problems in a small region (just the example, or the example and the accompanying prompt) is much easier than finding problems across a larger region; since finding problems in a sequence requires understanding the implications of all the examples in the sequence; (b) naturally occurring explanations are not always written in order of increasing difficulty because of other pragmatic factors (for instance, descriptions are often constrained by convention, by task, or other constraints such as temporal ordering, etc. Users are therefore apt to overlook this source of errors unless specifically trained to do so. In the example shown here, 10 of the 16 users did not find the problematic example in Fig. C.7.

These observations, although preliminary, suggest that such an interface can be very helpful in finding certain types of KB errors. It is clear that a more extensive and controlled evaluation is necessary before the actual value of such an interface can be determined. We hope to be able to conduct such an evaluation in the future, when we extend and evaluate the system with a set of much larger KBs in various domains that have been developed as part of other projects. Note that this approach to specification debugging is most effective in complex domains, where the specifications are abstract and concept specifications are highly interrelated. Domains that are characterized by a collection of simpler rules, such as "Ships cannot berth in ports less than X feet deep" may not benefit as much from this approach. For these domains, a purely textual description of the underlying KB structures, as in the EXPECT project (Gil, 1994) may be equally effective.

The experimental extension discussed this chapter can be easily tested in other domains. By using the BNF notation for representing the specifications, it is clear that, at the very least, domains that can be represented using BNF-like notation can be used with this framework. This approach scales well if the domain is represented using hierarchical relationships since the system can generate text and examples focused at higher, more abstract levels; thus any subconcepts below this level are assumed correct unless indicated otherwise.

C.4   Discussion

The verification of the accuracy of domain representation in large KBs is a difficult problem. A visual inspection of complex terms, abstract definitions and their inter-relationships may miss some of the more intricate boundary problems in the representation. This experiment has presented one approach to alleviating this problem. The scenarios presented here illustrate how some *mistakes in the original, abstract specification can be difficult to see, but can be made much more obvious when presented using suitable examples.* Based on the discourse plan underlying the presentation, the system attempts to localize the problem in the specification.

An important advantage of this approach, as compared to previous work on example based debugging (Shapiro, 1983; Mitchell, Utgoff, and Banerji, 1983) is the use of the goal structure in the discourse plan to localize the possible problems in the KB. Just indicating whether an example is correct or incorrect does *not* give as much leverage as being able to state that a specific example *in a series of other, coordinated, correct examples* is wrong. Another advantage of this approach is that it allows the system to address the issue of examples that only *look* correct (syntactically correct examples generated from a faulty specification for the wrong reasons–the reasons being indicated by prompts). Finally, the NL-based interface is more intuitive than the programmatic specification language; the domain expert debugging the KB need not be an expert in the KR specification language as well.

The work described in this chapter, and more broadly in the book, has focused on the use of examples in describing concepts, rather than relations or processes. The acquisition and representation of knowledge for these two categories using examples is much more complex and an area for future work.

Appendix D

Sample Descriptions in LISP Planned by the System

This appendix contains the concept descriptions that were planned by the system. These descriptions were selected at random from from the LISP domain rather than the INTEND domain since the LISP descriptions presented here can be compared with naturally occurring texts on LISP to gain some idea of the system's strengths and limitations. As we have stated earlier (in section 9.3), the current implementation does not have the semantics of the construct represented; this results in an inability to generate useful examples where the semantics are required. However, the current implementation does reason explicitly about the effects of the examples on the discourse, and effects such as the positioning of the examples and the order of presentation of the examples are taken into account.

Most of the descriptions given here are relatively straightforward. These descriptions suggest both the range and the limitations of the current implementation. They do not contain the typical uses of the function forms, nor give examples of what these forms might return if they executed (that could have been represented manually as an annotation, but was not). Some of these forms also display how the lack of a semantic representation can cause the generation of erroneous examples: for instance, the description of the REDUCE function resulted in two of the four examples being wrong.

The cons-form:

The construct CONS consists of a left parenthesis followed by the word CONS followed by a data element. Then there is a list and finally a right parenthesis. For example:

```
(CONS 'ORANGES '(PIZZAS APPLES CARS))
(CONS '2 '(PIZZAS APPLES CARS))
(CONS '(A B) '(PIZZAS APPLES CARS))
(CONS '(A B) '(3 PIZZAS 5 APPLES))
```

The car-form:

The construct CAR consists of a left parenthesis followed by the word CAR followed by a list followed by a right parenthesis. For example:

```
(CAR '(ORANGES MONKEYS CARS))
(CAR '(2 6 1 5 6))
(CAR '(ORANGES 2 CARS 6))
(CAR '((ORANGES ORANGES) (CARS MONKEYS)))
```

The cdr-form:

The construct CDR consists of a left parenthesis followed by the word CAR followed by a list followed by a right parenthesis. For example:

```
(CDR '(FISHES CARS APPLES CARS))
(CDR '(3 5 6))
(CDR '(MEN 7 CARS 7))
(CDR '((FISHES MEN) (ORANGES CARS)))
```

The function-form:

The function form consists of a left parenthesis followed by the word
DEFUN followed by a function name which is a symbol followed by a
parameter list which is a list of symbols. Then there is a body which
consists of zero or more s-expressions, followed by a right parenthesis.
For example:

```
(DEFUN ORANGES (MEN CATS PIZZAS)
       FISHES)
(DEFUN CARS (ORANGES FISHES)
       5)
(DEFUN FISHES (ORANGES MEN)
       (MEN CARS CARS))
```

The parameter list can have optional and keyword parameters in it.
Optional parameters are specified by the word &OPTIONAL. For example:

```
(DEFUN FISHES (&OPTIONAL CARS)
       MEN)
(DEFUN CARS (&OPTIONAL MEN PLANES CARS FISHES)
       PLANES)
```

Keyword parameters are specified by the word &KEY. For example:

```
(DEFUN FISHES (&KEY PLANES)
       CARS)
(DEFUN MONKEYS (&KEY MEN CARS ORANGES APPLES)
       PLANES)
```

The parameter list can have both optional and keyword parameters.
For example:

```
(DEFUN APPLES (&OPTIONAL ORANGES &KEY GRAPES)
       MONKEYS)
```

The prog-form:

The prog-form consists of a left parenthesis followed by the word PROG followed by a list of variables. There are some forms after the list of variables. Finally there is a right parenthesis. For example:

```
(prog (oranges) fishes aardvarks)
(prog (men blue) 2 3 4 5)
(prog (cars women apples) oranges 6 apples 7)
(prog (yellow fishes) (fishes men planes))
```

The constant-form:

A constant-form consists of either T, NIL, a number, or a quoted s-expression. For example:

```
T
NIL
5
'(fishes men)
'oranges
```

However, the following example is not a constant, but a variable because there is no quote:

```
oranges
```

The difference between a variable and a constant is that the value of a constant cannot be changed.

The append-form:

The append form consists of a left-parenthesis followed by the word APPEND followed by two lists. Finally there is a right parenthesis. For example:

```
(append '(oranges fishes) '(cars bananas))
(append '(1 3 5 7) '(cars planes))
(append '(oranges 3 men 5) '(fishes men cars))
(append '((cars men) (pizzas women)) '(aardvarks))
```

The reduce-form:

The reduce-form consists of a left parenthesis followed by a function name followed by a list. Finally there is a right parenthesis. The function name specifies a function that has two arguments. For example:

```
(reduce 'cons '(oranges pizzas men))
(reduce 'plus '(4 5 9 5 6))
(reduce 'times '(fishes 4 bicycles 9))
(reduce 'append '(cars planes (aardvarks aardvarks)))
```

(The last two examples assume that certain things are true: the variables fishes *and* bicycles *need to have numeric values; the variables* cars *and* planes *need to have values that are lists for the example to work.)*

The subset-form:

The subset-form consists of a left parenthesis followed by the word SUBSET followed by a unary predicate. This is followed by a list of elements and a right parenthesis. For example:

```
(SUBSET 'ODDP '(men cars planes))
(SUBSET 'NUMBERP '(fishes 2 oranges 7))
(SUBSET 'LISTP '((FISHES BLUE) (RED MEN)))
```

The let-form:

The let-form consists of a left parenthesis followed by the word LET followed by a list of local variables followed by a number of forms. Finally, there is a right parenthesis. A local variable is specified as a list

of the variable name which is a symbol and an initial value. Examples
of let-forms are:

```
(LET ((ORANGES FISHES)) MEN)
(LET ((BICYCLES 3) (PIZZAS 'MEN)) 2 9 CARS)
(LET ((YELLOW SKY) (FISHES BLUE)) (MEN AARDVARKS))
(LET ((APPLES APPLES) (FISHES SHARKS))
     ((MEN CARS) (MEN BLUE)))
```

(The last example illustrates the necessity of representing some of
the semantics in addition to the syntax: it has an erroneous declaration
of the local variable APPLES, since the variable will not have an initial
value, the assignment will give an error when executed.)

The setf-form:

The SETF-form consists of a list of three components: the keyword
SETF, followed by a variable name, followed by a value. The variable
name is a symbol; the value can be an expression. Examples of SETF-
FORMs are:

```
(SETF X23 3.1415)    ;  X23 is assigned the value 3.1415
(SETF BBB (A B C))   ;  BBB is assigned the value of the
                     ;       expression (A B C)
(SETF BAD ORANGES)   ;  BAD is assigned the value of ORANGES
```

However, the following is not a valid SETF-form because it cannot be
used to change the value of a constant or a number:

```
(SETF 123 ORANGES)   ;  invalid example, because 123 is not
                     ;       a variable
(SETF ABC 908)       ;  invalid example if ABC is a constant
```

The assoc-form:

The ASSOC-form is written as a list with three components: the keyword ASSOC, followed by a constant or a variable, followed by a list or
a variable representing a list. For example:

```
(ASSOC 'B '(ORANGES PIZZAS))   ; constant and a list
(ASSOC ABC '(ORANGES PIZZAS))  ; variable and a list
(ASSOC ABC XYZ)                ; two variables
(ASSOC ABC 'XYZ)         ; invalid example because the
                         ; second parameter is not a list
```

The float-form:

Floating point numbers are written as either decimal-numbers or exponent-numbers. Decimal-numbers consist of a sequence of digits followed by a decimal point followed by some more digits. Exponent-numbers consists of an optional sign, followed by some digits, optionally followed a decimal point and more digits, followed by an exponent. Examples of floating point numbers are:

```
1.0      ;  a floating point number in decimal notation
0E0      ;  a floating point zero in scientific notation
-.1      ;  a negative floating point number
+.1      ;  a positive floating point number
0.0      ;  a floating point number in decimal notation
0.       ;  not a floating point number, but an integer
```

The open-file-form:

The WITH-OPEN-FILE form consists of a list with three components: the keyword WITH-OPEN-FILE, a list consisting of a variable name, a pathname and optional declarations, and finally, an expression. For example:

```
(with-open-file
    (abc "/home/mittal/lisp-init.lisp"
         :direction :input)
    nil)

(with-open-file
    (xyz "/home/paris/.login" :direction :output
         :if-exists :supersede) (a b c))

(with-open-file
    (xyz "/home/mittal/ees.lisp")            'DONE)
```

However, the following is not a valid WITH-OPEN-FILE form because instead of a variable, it has a number as a parameter.

```
(with-open-file (453 "/home/mittal/ees.lisp") 'DONE)
```

The defstruct-form:

The DEFSTRUCT form consists of a list as follows: the first element of the list is the keyword DEFSTRUCT, followed by a NAME-EXPRESSION. This can be followed by an optional documentation string. The remaining elements consist of SLOT-DESCRIPTORS. The NAME-EXPRESSION can be either a symbol, or a list consisting of a name and optional keyword arguments. Each SLOT-DESCRIPTOR consists of a slot-name, optionally followed by default values. For example:

```
(defstruct ABC
    XYZ)                    ; a DEFSTRUCT form with name
                            ;    ABC and one slot XYZ
(defstruct BGF
    "Oranges Fishes"
    MMM GGG)                ; a DEFSTRUCT form with name
                            ;    BGF, two slots and a
                            ;    documentation string
(defstruct (GF56)
    GGG XYZ)                ; a defstruct form with name GF56
                            ;    and two slots
```

```
(defstruct (VIB
   :conc-name nil)
   YYY)                    ; a DEFSTRUCT form with the keyword
                           ;    argument :CONC-NAME defined
(defstruct (GAD
   :predicate "CHECK"
   :constructor "HHH")
   LKJ)                    ; a DEFSTRUCT form with two keyword
                           ;    arguments defined
```

The defconstant-form:

The DEFCONSTANT form consists of a list with the keyword DEF-
CONSTANT, followed by a variable-name, followed by a lisp expression
and finally followed by an optional documentation string. For example:

```
(defconstant ABC 453)
(defconstant R2D2 '(A 6 7 B))
(defconstant XYZ 567 "this is a string")
```

However, the following expression would be an invalid example of a
DEFCONSTANT-form:

```
(defconstant 456   '(a b c))
```

because 456 is not a valid variable name. Another invalid example of a
DEFCONSTANT-form is:

```
(defconstant (list (a b c)) 711)
```

This is because (list (a b c)) is not a variable name. The difference
between a DEFCONSTANT-form and a SETF-form is that the second
element of the list must be a variable name in DEFCONSTANT-form.

(Author note: Actually, a SETF-form and DEFCONSTANT-form differ
in another way as well: a SETF-form cannot have a documentation
string; the system did not detect it here because it tried to classify a
modified version of the last example and was successful with the SETF-
form.)

The dotimes-form:

The DOTIMES-form consists of a list with the following components: the keyword DOTIMES, followed by the ITERATION-LIST, followed by PROGN-BLOCK.[1] The ITERATION-LIST consists of a variable name and a lisp expression, which is not a quoted constant. [2] For example:

```
(dotimes (abc 4) <some lisp code here>)
(dotimes (r2d2 (a b c d)) <some lisp code here>)
(dotimes (b xyz) <some lisp code here>)

(dotimes (b 'xyz)              ; not a dotimes-form
    <some lisp code here>)     ;     since lisp-expression
                              ;     in ITERATION-LIST
                              ;     cannot be a quoted-
                              ;     constant
```

The endp-form:

The ENDP form consists of a list with two components: the keyword ENDP followed by a list or a variable. For example:

```
(ENDP  (A B C))       ; example of ENDP with a list
(ENDP  XYZ)           ; example of ENDP with variable
(ENDP  'ABC)          ; invalid example, since 'ABC is
                      ;     not a list nor a variable
(ENDP  NIL)           ; example of ENDP with a list
(ENDP  (AB) (CD))     ; invalid example because number
                      ;     of arguments must be one
```

---

[1] In many Lisp constructs, the body of the code is not essential — our system currently indicates these segments of code as PROGN-blocks.

[2] The initial representation of the DOTIMES-block omitted the result-form, an optional part of the specification that cannot be explained purely syntactically.

Author Index

Subject Index